HOW BIG
LITTLE THINGS CAN BE

HOW BIG
LITTLE THINGS CAN BE
Little is much when God is in it.

Frank Garlock

MAJESTY MUSIC®

Editor: Grace Collins Hargis
Cover design: Dwight Reid
Book layout: David Bonikowsky

Published by
SierraCreation
www.sierracreation.com

Donalds, South Carolina

ACKNOWLEDGMENTS AND GRATITUDE

At the outset of this book, I want to mention people who have come to my memory because of the influence each one has had on me. I am sure many of them would have thought what they did were just *little things*, but they were all *big things* for me. There are so many people who have influenced me over the years that a whole book could be written just about them and the way their lives have touched mine. I am sure there are many more who should be in this list, but here are just a few of those people:

- My own father and mother, who both showed great love to me and believed that I could do something worthwhile with my life—from the time I was born until they each went to be with their Lord at the age of 89

- Grandma Campbell, my mother's mother, who led me to the Lord when I was just five years old and then inspired Mrs. Cook to pay my way through BJU

- My older sister, Eunice, who was my best friend as a teenager and who prayed for me every day until she went to be with her Lord. At her memorial service on December 12, 2014, my youngest brother, Vic, quoted Isaiah 55:12: "For ye shall go out with joy, and be led forth with peace." He also said that "more than anyone else . . . Eunice was an example of Christian love and sacrifice for the rest of us."

- The kind ladies who ran the Verona Women's League and even hired a bus company to pick us up and take us to the house where they fed us poor kids hot lunches

- Edmund Schill, my first trombone teacher, who started me on the right path, took me to places where I could learn to play in front of people and didn't complain when I forgot to empty the "spit valve" before I played in some of those places

- The people and the pastor of the Caldwell Baptist Church, who let me play my trombone along with the congregational singing when I was just ten years old and didn't complain about my mistakes as I was learning to improvise on the instrument

- The many music teachers who took an interest in me and encouraged me to develop my talents, including the judges who accepted me into the New Jersey All-State High School Orchestra when I was just 13 years old

- The members of the New York Philharmonic, who took an interest in me at the Mountain Lakes Orchestra in New Jersey where I was playing and worked to get me a scholarship at Julliard School of Music that I never used because I came to BJU instead

- Evangelist Elmer Piper, John Piper's uncle, who made the original contact for me, and told me about the university in glowing terms so that I decided to go to Bob Jones University just two weeks before I came to the place of God's calling for me so I could learn to serve Him

- Elma Cook, who generously paid my way through college one month at a time and never complained because I became a minister of music and not a pastor

- Dr. Bob Jones, Sr., whose preaching convicted me and at the same time stirred up my desire to serve the Lord, which has stayed with me for almost 70 years now

- Eastman School of Music professor Elvera Wonderlich, who realized I could be a music theory teacher before I even thought of it and encouraged me to follow through with it

- Emory Remington, who gave me the background and knowledge I needed to be a trombone teacher and establish a trombone choir along with the brass quintet at BJU that is now the Foundation Brass Ensemble

- Arthur Kraft, who was a master voice teacher at Eastman and encouraged me to develop my "useful voice" for the Lord and sing in the excellent group called the Eastman Singers

- Dolphus Price, the pastor of Brent Baptist Church, who showed me how to work with ordinary people and had faith in me that I did not have, even making me the principal of the Brent Christian School in Pensacola

- Dwight Gustafson, who saw potential in me, invited me to teach at BJU, opened up my vision in several areas, and gave me my first opportunities to conduct operas

- Arlin and Beka Horton, who trusted me to teach the master's degree program in Sacred Music at Pensacola Christian College that gave me influence far beyond my expectations

- All the editors and proofreaders, and especially Grace Collins Hargis, who helped to make the books I have written look as if I knew what I was doing

- Shelly, Randy, and Gina, my own children who have stood with me and not complained about all the hours that I helped other people

- Ron and Shelly Hamilton, who had the courage to come work with me at Majesty Music and have used their talents to make the ministry effective in many areas that I never could have done

- My wife, Flora Jean, who has been my sustaining companion and my encourager through all the trials and opportunities that have come my way over the last 67 years

- The Lord Jesus Christ himself, who has never failed me, but has allowed me to love and serve Him in spite of all the failures and the mistakes that I have made

TABLE OF CONTENTS

Dr. Grace Collins Hargis

There is something about this book that everyone who reads it needs to understand. I wanted to say it was co-authored by Dr. Hargis and myself, but her humility would not accept that concept. She still wanted to be called my "editor."

I do not believe this extraordinary scholar and colleague could ever realize the effect she has had on my thinking for almost 50 years. I did not begin trying to be a writer until I was about 40 years old. Dr. Hargis has had a part in all the fifteen books and pamphlets that I have written without her even being aware that of what was always happening. The first book she edited for me was *The Big Beat: A Rock Blast* that was published in 1971. Her invaluable advice and counseling on that book has not only helped me in everything that I have written since then, it has also enabled me to sharpen the speaking that I have done for the same period of time.

For instance, in giving lectures on music and Biblical principles, I would sometimes be inaccurately questioned about something that I had said. My reply would be: "I can tell you exactly what I said, because Grace Collins Hargis helped me work that out and I have what I said memorized." This very often helped me to defend the position I had presented when I was challenged.

I need to go further and say that I believe Dr. Hargis has had more of an influence on my overall thinking process than any teacher I have ever had. Her uncanny ability along with her training and then teaching linguistics has enabled her to penetrate through my fuzzy reasoning and help me to say and write what I am actually thinking. To paraphrase what a famous author said about one of his books: "without her help this book would have been published upside down."

I want to personally thank my amazing friend for helping this musician, and that is my main field of endeavor, to write and speak like I know what I am doing. I should add here that I am very much aware that what God has enabled me to do for Him, especially in speaking and writing, has been with Grace's help. Most people do not expect a professional musician to be a writer or communicator. Her assistance has opened doors for me that I never could have had any other way.

I have often said that a person does not need a lot of close friends, but he does need some. Jim and Grace Hargis are that kind of friends to my wife, Flora Jean, and me, and we thank the Lord every day that our paths have crossed theirs.

INTRODUCTION

At the beginning of this book, I must admit that I am still struggling in becoming all that God wants me to be. I do fairly well in the big challenges of life, but I absolutely fail in the *little things*. Our wonderful, almighty God, the God of the Bible, is incomparable in both areas, big and small.

Many Christians like me miss much of what God wants us to know through His Word because we gloss over *little things*. For instance, let's consider phrases such as what the Bible says about water. Many of these phrases are in our language today. Jacob said that his eldest son, Reuben, was "unstable as water" (Genesis 49:4). When the Israelites were defeated at the battle of Ai, Joshua 7:5 says, "the hearts of the people melted, and became as water." When a wise woman was sent to David as Joab "put the words in her mouth" to trick the king, she said, "[We] are as water spilt on the ground, which cannot be gathered up again" (2 Samuel 14:14). The wisdom of Solomon in Proverbs says that a foolish woman tempts a man who lacks understanding by saying "stolen waters are sweet" (Proverbs 9:17).

Water is just one subject, but there are many Bible phrases that seem to be *little things* yet probably have more meaning than we sometimes realize. Job said, "I have escaped with the skin of my teeth" (Job 19:20); David said about Solomon, "His enemies shall lick the dust" (Psalm 72:9); Jesus said to His disciples about the Pharisees, "Let them alone: they be blind leaders of the blind" (Matthew 15:14); and Jesus admonished the scribes and Pharisees concerning the woman taken in adultery, "He that is without sin among you, let him first cast a stone at her" (John 8:7). There is also the admonition that we should all heed: "Pride goeth before destruction, and an haughty spirit before a fall" (Proverbs 16:18).

There are many more phrases that could be mentioned. However, I trust this book will help its readers to be aware of God's presence in every aspect of life and will cause us all to constantly thank our Lord for the many *little things* that our almighty, omniscient Father does for us every moment of our lives. I should also say here that I use personal illustrations on purpose, alternating them with Biblical ones, to show some things that God has taught me and is still teaching me about Himself. This is a life-long quest that will never be exhausted; He is so great that several lifetimes would not be long enough to learn everything there is to know about Him.

Devotions with "Little Things"

After completing this book, it was realized that it could be used as a devotional book for an individual, a family, or even a Sunday school class. Since there are 52 chapters, it could be a spiritual growth project for a year, one chapter each week, alternating what the Bible says one week and applying the principle to life the next week.

Since the author of the book alternated chapters by using the odd numbered chapters for a Bible principle and then applying it to his own life with illustrations in the even numbered chapters, the same thing could be done with two or more people. The individual's experience does not need to match what the author experienced. It can be used wherever an opportunity arises.

Here are a few suggestions for family devotions:

1. Read the chapter with the odd number and meditate on what it says for a week. (Look up Vignette #13 in Just Show Up: God Can Use You)

    *   Try memorizing a key verse that teaches the principle involved.

- Print out the first letters of the verse(s) to help memorization.

- Practice quoting the verse(s) together.

- Discuss what each family member is learning with the whole family.

2. The following week apply the principle learned to your lives, and how each person helped someone else

   - Each one share with the family how he or she applied what was learned the previous week.

   - Encourage each other by praying for individual growth.

   - Thank each other for sharing personal experiences.

These suggestions could be applied to a couple, to a Sunday school class, or to any other group that wants to experience spiritual growth.

Chapter 1

KNOWLEDGE AND WISDOM

The impetus for this book came to me with the realization that my wonderful, all-powerful God has included many *little things* in His Word that usually go unnoticed. He has also done so many *little things* in my own life that I have too often taken for granted. Therefore, the basic format for this book is to alternate between *little things* that the Bible reveals and events of my own life that show God's interest in *little things*.

I realize that a few things I write for this book have been mentioned in one of my other books. However, I believe that illuminating some of those will help my readers understand how God in so many cases used *little things* to accomplish His will both in the Scripture and in my life.

At the ripe old age of 88, I must still take the necessary time to practice what I have preached for many years. When the Lord wakes me up in the middle of the night (which I understand is usual for people my age), I not only go through some of the prayer lists that I have kept for about 60 years now; I also take the time to *meditate* on Scriptural passages that I have memorized (see Vignette 13 of my book *Just Show Up: God Can Use You* where I explain the details of Biblical meditation).

I suppose the most frequently used and yet one of the most remarkable Psalms in the Bible is Psalm 23. It has been the most quoted, referred to, cherished, and misunderstood passage in the Bible. Take, for instance, the first phrase of that Psalm: "The LORD is my shepherd." Think about the measureless import of the three main words of that phrase: "LORD," "my" and "shepherd." Meditation on just those three words can occupy your thinking for a long time.

I will come back to some of my meditation on those three words later in this book, but at this point, let me mention two books that every reader of this book should have in his library. The first one is by one of my favorite authors, W. Philip Keller. He authored at least 50 books and I have many of them in my library, including *Lessons from a Sheep Dog* and *A Layman Looks at the Lamb of God*. However, my favorite is his best-known book, *A Shepherd Looks at Psalm 23*. If you have never read that book or if you have not read it in a long time, the reading of it will help you to understand the purpose of this book.

The following may be an overstatement, but I will venture to say that the sheep concept is one of the keys to understanding many things in the Bible, including the birth and death of Christ. The Lamb of God was born when lambs are born in Israel, and He died when the lambs are sacrificed. A thorough knowledge of this concept opens the mind of a student of the Word of God to the purposes of God in a myriad of instances. My desire is to reveal many of these instances in this book along with my own personal encounters with God's purposes in my own life.

The second book I want to mention is a recent one: *More Than Meets the Eye: Fascinating Glimpses of God's Purpose and Design* by Richard Swenson, M.D. Dr. Swenson not only is a medical doctor, but he also has a degree in biophysics that enables him to explore the "design of science" in order to understand "the Designer who stands behind it all." This book will begin to open your eyes and heart to the overwhelming conceptualization of the omnipotent God who created and sustains everything including the trillions of subatomic particles (infinitesimal things) that reveal that God has creative abilities that go far beyond our comprehension. This book was first published in the year 2000 and the reading of it will help you realize how little we really know about our awesome Almighty God.

I would also like to illustrate the principle we are discussing with a practical application. The Bible makes it clear in many places that there is a tremendous difference between knowledge and wisdom. As James wrote in his book: "If any of you lack *wisdom*, let him ask of God" (James 1:5). Notice that it does not say "knowledge." As someone has wisely said: "Knowledge is knowing that a tomato is a fruit. Wisdom is understanding that it does not belong in a fruit salad." The distinction makes a difference in the application.

So come with me as we begin to explore *little things* in the Bible and how the Lord has used so many of them in my life. My hope is that reading these things will open your mind and heart to understand how He has worked in your life as well, so that you can properly thank Him for His goodness and kindness to you.

I want to quote from a song I wrote in 1984 called "The God of the Impossible." It is number 75 in *Majesty Hymns* if you want to look it up, but here is the first stanza and chorus:

> *I don't know how God hangs the world on nothing,*
> *Or how He keeps the planets each in place.*
> *I cannot count the sands upon the seashore,*
> *Nor can I count the stars that float in space.*
>
> *But God can do what seems impossible;*
> *God controls eternity.*
> *My mind can never comprehend it,*
> *But God in heaven cares for me.*

When God wants to do something good, He starts with the difficult. When He wants to do something great, He starts with the impossible!

Chapter 2

1500 Miles Apart

This may seem like a strange place to begin the chapters about how God has worked many *little things* in my life, but I think it is probably the best place to start, and I hope you will agree after you read this chapter.

I was born in Montclair, New Jersey, on August 10, 1930, in what was called the Montclair Community Hospital. I was number four of nine children, and because of the meager finances even at that time in the family, my mother had to go to a clinic to receive whatever treatment she could get for the pregnancy of her fourth child.

I was told by my parents that there was some problem while I was in my mother's womb. They said the doctor at the clinic told them that they would probably lose me along the way. They also told me that they dedicated me to the Lord at that point, and they promised Him that if I survived, they would dedicate me to serve Him in some special way. By God's grace I survived, and when they brought me home and put me in the carriage someone had given them, I was so long that my head hit the top and my feet hit the bottom of the carriage. My mother also mentioned that she was glad that I was born on Sunday, because she somehow knew I was going to serve the Lord.

At this point, I should also mention that my mother's father, Grandpa Campbell, who was opposed to his only daughter having four children in just five years, still said I was the most beautiful baby he had ever seen. Grandpa Campbell did show me a lot of love, so that I distinctly remember him and my grandmother taking me to a store to buy me a sharp little sailor outfit when I was five years old. Little did my grandparents know that five more children would come along so that the oldest and youngest of the nine would be born exactly 18 years apart on January 12.

Pa would also cut my hair with his manual hair-cutting tool. I am glad that he would not complain when I hollered because that hair-cutter would pull the hairs out by the roots instead of cutting them. He did that even into my teenage years. One day he went to the local barber and asked him to cut my hair for fifteen cents instead of a quarter to save the family some needed money.

There was no way that my family or Flora Jean's family could have known two and a half months after I was born that the beautiful baby girl the Lord gave them would someday be the one that God had prepared for me. Flora Jean was born in Okeene, Oklahoma, on October 25, 1930, in the small farmhouse in which her family lived.

Her parents told us years later that her mother had been told that she would probably lose that baby because of some problems in the pregnancy. Sam and Leuvina Fox, hearing that message, dedicated themselves and the baby to the Lord's service in whatever way He would choose. Again, there was no way the Foxes could have known what a special girl the Lord was giving them, and how the talents He was giving her would be used for His glory.

Living on a wheat farm outside of a very small town in Oklahoma would not seem like a place where a talented girl would ever use those talents. But Flora Jean loved the piano. So she started practicing at age four because she says "she had nothing else to do" except pluck chicken feathers, herd cattle, and milk cows. She listened to the only one she admired for his talent in playing hymns and gospel songs, Rudy Atwood of the Old-Fashioned Revival Hour radio program. However, she developed her own unique style during those formative years, and she has taught those techniques in the places where the Lord has called us and in more than fifty countries where we have served the Lord through music.

In a later chapter, I will tell how Flora Jean and I knew on our first date together during Bible Conference week at BJU in 1951 that we were destined for each other. But let me just say here that there was no question in either of our minds or hearts that we were meant to serve the Lord *together*! Every *little thing* that we talked about that day confirmed to each of us that God had planned from the foundation of the earth to bring Frank Garlock and Flora Jean Fox together by His grace, and we have never doubted it in the more than 66 years that we have been married.

Chapter 3

A SHEPHERD'S CARE

One of the things that make us so much like sheep is not realizing how *little things* can affect so much of what we do and how we live. If a sheep does not get enough exercise and becomes fat or if it grows too much wool on its body, both the sheep and the shepherd have a problem. A shepherd wants his sheep to be strong, sturdy, and energetic; not fat, flabby, and weak.

This is similar to what the shepherd David was talking about in Psalm 42:5, 11 and in Psalm 43:5 when he said: "Why art thou *cast down*, O my soul?" This expression "cast down" reminds us of a cast sheep. A cast sheep is one that has turned over on its back and cannot get up again by itself.

There are three basic things that can happen to sheep to cause them to be cast. These same things can happen to God's children. Number one is that the sheep are looking for soft spots to lie down. Wherever sheep are grazing, there are always soft places where sheep can be comfortable and just take it easy. They do not move around with the other sheep that are keeping themselves trim and active. In the soft place, it is easy for the sheep to roll over and become cast and helpless. The shepherd must come and rescue that cast sheep.

The spiritual application is obvious. God does not want His children to always look for soft places where there is no hardship that requires self-discipline. We often equate financial security, a nice home, an expensive car, or a lofty position in a community with God's blessing. That's why Jesus said in Luke 12:15, "Take heed, and beware of covetousness: for a man's life consisteth not in the abundance of things which he possesseth." And the Apostle Paul in 1 Corinthians 10:12 said, "Wherefore let him that thinketh he standeth take heed lest he fall [be cast]."

The second thing that can cause a sheep to be cast is simply having too much wool on its body. The sheep is literally weighed down with its own wool. The wool becomes heavily matted with mud, manure, and all kinds of other things that are keeping the sheep from doing what it should, and the heavy wool can very easily cause the sheep to be cast.

For the Christian, this is being preoccupied with self. It is the accumulation of things and possessions that we think are making us comfortable. Actually, these things are weighing us down and keeping us from being effective as we try to serve our Savior. That is when the Good Shepherd has to come along and get us out of the place where we are cast. He must take us back to the sheepfold and shear off the extra wool that is hindering us from being all that God wants us to be. We will not, as God's sheep, like the shearing any more than they do, but it has to be done.

As I am writing this, I am experiencing some shearing by God. He has allowed me to come into some conditions that are not pleasant. But if God has allowed them to come, I am having to submit to the shearing without any questions and ask the Lord to help me not ask "why." I want to quote here a poem my grandmother wrote two and a half months before she went to be with her Lord at 75 years of age. I found it in her Bible and set it to music 20 years after she wrote it.

Lord, teach me how to worship Thee in spirit and in truth;
Teach me how to wait on Thee, and thus renew my youth.
Teach me how to mount above the burdens of the day;
Lord, teach me, oh, please teach me how to let Thee have Thy way.

The third thing that can cause sheep to be cast is for them to get too fat. Fat sheep are neither healthy nor productive. That extra weight puts too much stress on the body of the sheep and makes it easier to be in a rut and be cast. We could apply this to our country right now because being overweight physically is a real problem in the USA. The data from a recent National Health and Nutrition Survey states that "more than 2 in 3 adults are considered to be overweight or obese." One does not need to go very far to look around and see many people who need to lose weight.

I believe the spiritual problem among Christians is similar to the physical problem among the general population. Too many Christians are weak because they believe they have "arrived." When Christians become most sure of themselves is when they are in the greatest danger of being cast spiritually. Material success is no measure of spiritual health. Scripture tells us that God disciplines those He loves. Hebrews 12:6 says, "whom the Lord loveth He chasteneth." In this context I believe it could mean He has to shear us of things that will hinder us and make us cast and helpless. It is part of the price of belonging to our wonderful Shepherd, the Lord Jesus Christ.

Aren't you glad that we have His Word to guide and comfort us as His sheep? For instance, 1 Corinthians 10:13 says, "There hath no temptation taken you but such as is common to man: *BUT GOD IS FAITHFUL*, who will not suffer [allow] you to be tempted above that ye are able; but will *with the temptation* also make a way to escape [shear the wool off], that ye may be able to bear it." Too much of this world's goods is a temptation. But our Shepherd is faithful!

Chapter 4

BEING SENSITIVE
TO GOD'S LEADING

I am going to digress a little bit in this chapter because three things have happened during the week that I am writing this book that need to be mentioned here.

However, I want to start with a *little thing* that occurred two weeks ago that meant a lot to me. Bob Jones University was having a "Homecoming Celebration" that included many special events. One of those events was a BJU Symphony Orchestra Concert to which about 40 alumni were invited to participate. I was probably invited partially because I was a member of that orchestra in 1949, sixty-nine years ago.

One of the selections to be played was the *Festival Overture* by Dmitri Shostakovich. When I received the music, I was made aware that the trombone part for that piece is written in the alto clef where middle C in on the third line of the clef. Many trombonists never need to play in that clef, but I learned to do it as a teenager. The part moved ahead so rapidly that it was extremely difficult to keep up with it. However, by practicing a lot I was able to play it.

However, the most thrilling thing the night of the performance was not the playing of that piece. It was that sitting in that orchestra on the platform, I could see into the balcony of the auditorium, and I was looking at the two seats where Flora Jean and I had had our first date sixty-seven years ago. Tears came to my eyes that night as I was still able to play my trombone and see the very seats where the Lord brought our lives and desires together to serve our Savior for all these years!

The first of the other three things was a call this past Monday from David, our son-in-law who is married to our youngest daughter. He and Gina live in Navarre, Florida, where he is currently an inspector who determines whether a building is properly constructed to withstand the forces of the hurricanes that come to that part of the country. (See Chapter 26 of this book.)

He said he had done an inspection for an older lady several weeks ago and she had given him $100 to pay for the limited inspection. He then said that every time he was going to either cash the check or put it in the bank, God seemed to say, "don't do it." Finally, last Thursday, when he went to put the check in the bank, God more emphatically seemed to say, "send the check back to her!" It wasn't an audible voice, but David is sensitive to the Lord's leading, and he sent the check back.

When David called me on Monday, the woman had just contacted him to thank him for sending the check back. Number one, she needed the money. Number two, that day was her husband's and her 55th anniversary. However, he had passed away and this was her first anniversary without him. David was sensitive to God's leading and He used a *little thing* to prompt him to do a *big thing* for that lady.

Another example of David's heart came to light when David's daughter, Torie, was in nursing school. Torie had made special friends with a girl named Jenna, who was also in nursing school. They discovered that they were from the same area of Florida. One day while talking, Jenna told Torie the story of how her father had passed away and they were considering a move to Florida. While looking at houses, an inspector had prayed with her mom about moving there. Torie immediately responded. "That was probably my dad!!!" And it was! Torie has commented many times on what a blessing and sweet Christian friend that Jenna has been to her during her difficult years in nursing school.

On Tuesday of this week, I went to see Paul Wickensimer, a friend that I have known and with whom I have been on the Wilds Christian Camp board for many years. Paul is the Clerk of Court for the County of Greenville, SC, where we live. I was there to ask him if he could help me because of his position and obtain a document that I needed. He was able to do that, for which I am grateful.

However, he and I talked for about a half hour about many things including what I have just written. When I related the above to him, he said, "Let me tell you a thing that happened to me." I was eager to hear something from this man of God. He then told me that he had been in Atlanta for a meeting, and that when the meeting was delayed he went somewhere to get a Coke. As he was standing in front of the cashier, a woman was standing in front of the one next to him.

Paul is very sensitive to the leading of God, and the Lord seemed to prompt him to pay for the woman's lunch. His natural instinct was to resist because of what the woman might think. When the Lord seemed to prompt him the second time, he made another excuse to himself. When the prompt came the third time, he said to his cashier, "Put her lunch on my bill." The woman immediately said, "You don't need to do that. I have money."

But when Paul said that God had prompted him to do it, she said: "I will do it on one condition." Paul replied: "What is that?" She said: "If you will have lunch with me." When they sat down at a table, the woman began to cry. When Paul asked her why she was crying, she said: "Today is my husband's and my anniversary. But he died a year ago today and I asked the Lord to do something special for me. You just did it!"

On Wednesday of this week, I went to see a lawyer friend of mine to get some advice about a contract. This man, Charles (Chuck) Hofstra, is another man who loves the Lord and seeks to serve Him in many ways including the small fees he charges. When I related the two things mentioned above, he offered to tell me how he and his wife met at BJU. He was evidently a poor boy when he came to BJU and had only two pairs of corduroy pants just as I did when I came. He would alternate the pants and the few shirts he had so it looked like he had more clothes.

One day in the BJU snack shop, he saw a girl named Arlene and was so impressed with her that he wanted to ask her what her name was. But he was too bashful, and he had to request one of his friends to ask for her name. He told me he knew that day that someday she would be his wife, and they have now been happily married for forty-seven years and are serving the Lord through both their church and his law practice.

If you have read my book, *Just Show Up: God Can Use You*, check Vignette 30, where I discuss the Golden Triangle Principle and how that applies to what I have related here. The triangle, as any engineer will tell you, is a symbol of strength that is applied in buildings and bridges. It also demonstrates the strength and blessings that God gives us when we are sensitive to His leading in our lives. He uses things that seem *little* to us to do *big* things in the lives of others.

Chapter 5

SPARROWS AND EAGLES

I am definitely not an ornithologist, but I have always been interested in the nature of various birds and how God refers to them in His Word. It is so compelling to see how God uses creation to teach us things about Himself. That is why I have titled this chapter "Sparrows and Eagles" since those species are mentioned often in both the Old and the New Testaments.

For instance, in Psalm 84, which is about "longing and fainting" for the courts of the Lord, the sparrow is mentioned along with the swallow as an illustration of how we are to meditate on the blessedness of coming into God's presence and dwelling in God's house. The metaphor seems to refer to a little bird that is looking for a safe place to build a nest and to trust itself and its prize possession, its young, to the hand of God.

Jesus also selected the sparrow as a special concern of His Father in Matthew 10:29-31. He said, "one of them shall not fall on the ground without your Father ... [and] ye are of more value than many sparrows." In fact, the well-loved song, "His Eye Is on the Sparrow" is based upon those words of our Lord. Doctor Luke even remembers another thing that Jesus said about this story when he adds the phrase: "not one of them is forgotten before God" (Luke 12:4-7).

That brings us to another bird that the Bible mentions and that is one of my favorites, the eagle. In "The Song of Moses" in Deuteronomy 32, Moses refers to Jacob as the Lord's inheritance in verse 9, and then in verses 11-13 he graphically compares the Lord to an eagle that "stirs up her nest," and "bears [her young] on her wings," so that "the LORD alone did lead him" and "made him ride on the high places of the earth."

The picture here is what a mother eagle does for her brood. After an eaglet gets to a certain size or maturity, everything changes for the baby eagle! The next thing the mother eagle does is to push the little one out of the nest, and the eaglet falls down the face of the cliff, surely to be destroyed. But not so! In a flash the great mother eagle flies down, catches the little one on her back, and flies up and deposits it in the nest. The mother bird pushes the little one out again, and again, over and over.

Why would a mother do such a thing to her young? Does she hate the little one? Not at all! It's just that those little birds were made to fly, and they don't know it, so she is going to help them figure it out. She never lets them hit bottom, but she does let them fall, because she wants to teach them how to fly as an eagle should.

Isaiah 40:31 has always had a special place in my heart and in my service for the Lord since I was a member of the Basilean literary society as a student at Bob Jones University. Our sports teams were the Eagles, and our theme verse was "they that wait upon the LORD shall renew their strength; they shall mount up with wings *as eagles*;[1] they shall run, and not be weary; and they shall walk, and not faint." Ron Hamilton has written a beautiful and inspiring song with that verse as its theme.

We will examine the beak of an eagle in the next chapter of this book, but suffice it to say here that the Bible also refers to the eagle as an instrument of divine judgment on moral and spiritual corruption. Our Lord used the eagle as a metaphor in Matthew 24:28 and in Luke 17:37 as an image of the terrible consequences of the disobedience of man during the tribulation, when He said, "wheresoever the body is, thither will the eagles be gathered together."

A metaphor is one of the most extensively used literary devices, ascribing a meaning or identity to one subject by way of another. In a metaphor, one subject is implied to be another so as to draw a comparison between their similarities and shared traits. The eagle

---

1 You may be interested to view a record-setting flight from a camera fitted to the back of an eagle. The eagle was released from the top of the world's tallest building to search for his trainer, more than a half mile below. The eagle, released from the top of the 2,715-foot Burj Khalifa tower in Dubai, had no idea where the tiny speck of land was that his handler was standing on. Somehow from that altitude, the eagle actually sees and recognizes his handler in the midst of all of the other objects and people. In the video (minute 1:38) you can see him looking and looking for the trainer, completely invisible to a human eye and the camera, then fold his wings and power-dive directly to him. youtu.be/6g95E4VSfj0

is a perfect metaphor that God employs to show how eagles will be a part of the coming judgment that Christ reveals in His Olivet Discourse (Matthew 24:27-31).

There are 33 kinds of birds mentioned in the Bible, and God uses them in His Word to teach us lessons that will make us more effective in serving Him. God's attention to birds demonstrates again His concern for *little things*. There is much more that we could learn by studying birds and what God says about them in His Word.

Chapter 6

BIRD BEAKS

To try to demonstrate all the beaks of the more than 10,000 kinds of birds in the world would be an almost impossible task for an ornithologist, and an unthinkable task for a book like this one. However, I would like in this chapter to illustrate just a few of the myriad types of bird beaks there are to show how much God must be interested in *little things*.

The most important need of a bird is getting something to eat. Birds spend most of their days just looking for food. That is why God made each species with special equipment to eat what it needs to survive. There are nutcrackers, insect eaters, chisels, straws, fish eaters, fly catchers, hooks, and strainers, to name just a few of the *little things* that God placed in the beaks of birds when He created them. Some birds even use their beaks as "an extra hand" to climb, build nests, tie knots, feed their young, and groom themselves.

Let's begin with the small narrow oval beak of the hummingbird. It is very much like a straw that the hummingbird sticks into flowers to sip the nectar out of them as food for itself. Hummingbirds are also pollinators for transporting seeds and pollen to other flowers. And yet, their beak, which is longer than the hummingbird's body, is not really like a straw since it is not hollow. The lower beak is slightly flexible and can widen and bend lightly downward as the humming-birds open their mouths to suck in the nectar. They "dip and sip" with their long, needlelike beaks as they probe deep into flowers.

The pelican is mentioned three times in the Bible, and its use is one of the most fascinating ones in Psalm 102:6 where the psalmist in affliction compares himself to "a pelican in the wilderness." The American White Pelican is the largest aquatic bird in the world, and its huge beak measures up to 15.2 inches. The most interesting characteristic of their beak is that the lower mandible acts as a filter that helps them to catch fish and drain away the excess water. The merganser duck is also unusual in that it has a bill that is like a sleeve that drains water out on the sides as it catches fish.

Then there are herons that have beaks like a spear that they use to stab fish and lift them out of the water. The woodpecker's beak is like a chisel to drill holes into the bark of trees so they can get at the insects that are inside.

The eagle has a strong beak with a hooked upper jaw that it uses to tear flesh of any prey that it catches. On the other hand, the cardinal, like many other birds, has a short, stout conical beak that acts like a nutcracker to open seeds and nuts.

One of my favorite birds to study is the loon. Loons are swimming and diving birds. They have very distinctive bodies: long and low-slung with spear-like beaks. Common items on the loon's menu are perch, bullhead, and sunfish. They are also known to eat frogs, crayfish, and even leeches. The loon dives underwater to grab its prey with its beak and then swallows it in one gulp.

Remember, we are not talking about other things that birds can do. Beaks are just one of the amazing *little things* that demonstrate the intricate care our great God has taken with His wonderful creation.

However, to close this chapter, I must mention something that I just learned. The Wright Brothers were able to do what many others tried and failed to do by studying how God designed bird *wings*. Their notebooks include detailed notes on bird flight, particularly on the way bird wings are made. They believed that if a bird could effortlessly glide and its "wings could sustain it in the air without the use of any muscles, we do not see why man could not be sustained by the same means."[1]

This is just another illustration of the power of our great God and His interest in little things that can become big things. Very few men have changed the world the way the Wright brothers did, and they did it by studying a small part of the way God created things that we have mentioned here: birds' beaks and wings.

---

1 Moolman, V. *The Road to Kitty Hawk*. Time-Life
  Books, pp. 107-108. Alexandria, VA. 1980

Chapter 7

THE VOICE OF GOD

In this chapter, I hope to show my readers that what may seem like a *little thing* to us is actually a *big thing* in the mind of God. Jesus made this clear in the tenth chapter of the book of John. The Pharisees were constantly looking for ways to corner Him, and He uses the lesson of a shepherd and his sheep to show them how blind they are to spiritual truth. In fact, at the close of chapter nine, He says: "I am come . . . that they which see not might see; and that they which see might be made blind" (John 9:39).

There are several *little things* in this one chapter of the Word of God, but the *little thing* that I want to draw attention to here is the *voice* of the Son of God, and the emphasis that Jesus puts on it. Notice the phrases: "the sheep hear his voice: and he calleth his own sheep by name (v. 3); "the sheep follow him: for they know his voice" (v. 4); "they know not the voice of a stranger" (v. 5); "other sheep I have . . . them also I must bring, and they shall hear my voice" (v. 16); "my sheep hear my voice, and I know them, and they follow me" (v. 27).

Psalm 29 is basically a Psalm about the voice of the LORD. "The voice of the LORD is upon the waters" (v. 3); "powerful" (v. 4a); and "full of majesty" (v. 4b). It "breaks the cedars" (v. 5); "divides the flames of fire" (v. 7); "shakes the wilderness" (v. 8); "makes the hinds to calve" (v. 9a); and "discovers [uncovers] the forests" (v. 9b). Here in this one Psalm we learn eight important things about the voice of our Almighty God.

A quick trip through the Bible reveals how important the voice of God is. The first mention of His voice is in Genesis 3:8 where Adam and Eve "heard the voice of the Lord God" and they "hid themselves from [His] presence." There ensued then a conversation between the Lord and the first people on the earth. In reading this, we must remember that any time the Bible puts the word for Lord in all capital letters, it is referring to Jehovah, the Old Testament equivalent of Jesus in the New Testament. In other words, Jehovah is Jesus.

However, if we go back to the first chapter of Genesis, we learn of the powerful, overwhelming, almighty voice of God in Creation. Just as Genesis 1:1, like so many other Scriptures, uses an adumbration when it says, "In the beginning God," it does not attempt to prove or defend God; it just assumes God and presents what He did.

This is also true concerning the "voice of God" in Genesis 1 and 2. Scripture simply states, "God said" at least ten times in those chapters. God said, "let there be light: and there was light." God said, "let there be a firmament ... and it was so." God said, "Let there be lights in the firmament ... and it was so." These are only three of the times "God said" and it was done.

And that brings me to some of my favorite events that demonstrate the power of the voice of God. In Psalm 18, David recounts God's deliverance of him (2 Samuel 22) and says, "Then the earth shook and trembled ... because He was wroth." This is only one occasion of many in the Old Testament where God shook the earth with His voice.

The next reference to the voice of God that I want to mention is when God told Abraham that He would bless him and "all the nations of the earth" because Abraham obeyed His voice (Genesis 22:18). In contrast to this, when God evidently spoke to Pharaoh as Moses and Aaron talked to him, Pharaoh said: "Who is the LORD, that I should obey his voice ... I know not the LORD" (Exodus 5:2).

There is an intriguing event concerning the voice of God in Genesis 28 when Jacob is fleeing from the wrath of his brother Esau. While traveling toward Haran, he lies down at night and uses stones for a pillow. He then has his extraordinary dream in which he sees angels ascending and descending a ladder that reaches from earth to heaven. But then he sees God above the ladder *saying*, "I am the LORD God of Abraham thy father."

Jacob realizes who is talking to him, but the vow he makes at the end of this chapter is a strange one in that his commitment to God is conditional. His fuller commitment comes in Genesis 32 after he wrestles with God and his name is changed from Jacob (the deceiver) to Israel (strength).

The book of Deuteronomy is very interesting in this regard—this one book of the Bible mentions the voice of the LORD twenty-eight times. This should reveal to anyone who is eager to obey God and to find His will that he should be listening for the voice of God. As I mentioned in Chapter 4 of this book, God does not normally speak audibly to us, but when we are sensitive to His leading, His Spirit often prompts us to obey Him. The book of Deuteronomy points out that God is listening to our voices by mentioning that God was listening to the Israelites five times in that book.

The very next advent of the voice of the LORD is in 1 Samuel 3. Here we read of how God spoke to young Samuel "ere the lamp of God went out . . . and Samuel was laid down to sleep; that the LORD called Samuel" three times before Samuel finally realized who was calling him. In fact, the third time God called Samuel, the Scripture in verse 10 says that "the LORD came and *stood* and *called* as at other times . . . Then Samuel answered, Speak, for thy servant heareth." This is one special time when God actually spoke to a young boy in an audible voice. God's voice was so clear to Samuel that he thought it was the priest Eli who was calling him. Would that all of us could be like Samuel at whatever age God speaks to us.

But in the New Testament there are several more times when God speaks and the earth shakes. At the cross of Christ just after He gave up His life, "the earth did quake . . . the centurion "saw the earthquake" and said, "Truly this was the Son of God" (Matthew 27). And then in Matthew 28 the angel came and rolled back the giant stone from the tomb with an earthquake.

The passage that most reveals to me the power of God's voice is in Acts 16. Paul and Silas had been beaten and put in prison for preaching the gospel. They were "thrust into the inner prison" where their feet, and perhaps their hands, were made fast in the stocks. But when "Paul and Silas prayed and sang praises unto God . . . there was a great earthquake ... and immediately all the doors were opened and everyone's bonds were loosed."

Now this was an unbelievable earthquake. I believe it was not a *little thing* because of how unusual it was. Just think about it! It was a *local* earthquake, unlike the one I was in in Haiti in 2010. Apparently only the prison was affected. The doors of the prison were opened, and everyone's bands (chains) were loosed. That is not a usual earthquake! In other words, I believe the voice of God did it for Paul and Silas so that the jailor could come to know their Savior.

We all should be sensitive to the voice of God in our lives. It is not normally an audible voice. It might be like an earthquake, or just an event that God uses to make us aware of His presence and to make us receptive to whatever God desires for us to do. May we all be like young Samuel, who finally realized it was God speaking and said, "Speak; for thy servant heareth."

Chapter 8

THE POWER OF THE VOICE

I want to begin this chapter with something my mother said to me when I was young. I remember that there was one particular time when I reluctantly agreed to do something I really did not want to do. I don't remember what the actual event was, but I remember vividly what my mother said. In fact, I can still hear her saying it: "Frank, *don't talk to me in that tone of voice!*" What was a *little thing* to me was a *big thing* to my mother. Now, knowing my own stubborn will, I probably did not say anything bad that I should not have. But the manner in which I said it was what my mother understood very well, and she admonished me for it.

Another thing that stands out lucidly in my memory is what I would say to my siblings when I was a very young child. I am sure that the fact that I would say what I did was the reason my older siblings would enjoy teasing me about it. One of them would call my name, and when I would answer, their answer came back to me: "Nothing!" I would then say: *"I don't like that noise!"*

The two illustrations above are both really *little things*, but they were big to me. They also show what James 3:5-10 tells us: "The tongue is a little member, and boasteth great things. Behold, how great a matter a little fire kindleth . . . The tongue can no man tame." God evidently knew how much trouble our tongues (voices) could get us into when He included that warning in His Word.

However, the main thing I want to emphasize in this chapter is the power that God has given each of us in the unique voice that is ours alone. Technology has made many strides in this area since the 1960s. It is sometimes called speech recognition, voice detection, voice recognition, voiceprint identification, voice biometrics, or a number of other names.

Bell Laboratories began developing voice recognition in the 1940s, and by the 1960s the Michigan State Police adopted the technique. By 1967, five thousand law enforcement voice identification cases had been processed by certified voiceprint examiners. In a variety of criminal cases, voice analysis, along with acoustic analysis, has been used by voiceprint examiners to help solve criminal cases.

Science is recognizing that no two people who have ever lived have exactly the same voice that another person has. Similarly, no two people have the same DNA, no two of our nerve cells are exactly the same, and each neuron is unique in the whole universe. In fact, your initial single-cell DNA, which determines everything about you, only weighs 0.2 millionths of a millionth of an ounce. Some scientists believe that your DNA and your voice are closely related.

The fundamental theory behind all of this rests on the premise that every voice is individually characteristic so that each individual's voice can be identified through analysis. There are two general factors involved in determining voice uniqueness. The first is the size and shape of the mouth and the nasal cavity as well as the shape, length, and tension of the vocal cords. Evidently God has made each of us different enough that the possibility of two people being the same is very remote.

The second factor lies in the manner in which the muscles are formed while a person is speaking. Thus, the two factors include the lips, teeth, tongue, soft palate, and jaw muscles. The likelihood that two people could develop similar patterns is also very remote. In other words, God again, through His interest in *little things*, has made each person unique down to every detail of our bodies and beings.

Investigators have found through thorough research that even very good mimics cannot duplicate another person's speech patterns. Barclays, an international bank, is rolling out voiceprint identification for its 12 million banking customers. Just as fingerprinting is being used for authentication, voice printing can be used for the same purpose. Voice printing uses unique information about a person's vocal tract and the behavior of a person's speaking pattern.

Businesses and governments around the world are turning to voiceprints for all kinds of security practices. ValidSoft is a London-based vendor of this technology. At Vanguard in Pennsylvania, many customers log into their accounts by speaking the phrase: "At Vanguard, my voice is my password."

My final conclusion to this chapter is something I have been saying for more than forty-seven years when I have spoken about the problems with rock music. The words may be good. They may even be Biblical. But the sensual, loud, guttural sound, coupled with the

sensual beat, turns even Bible words into blasphemy. The *voice* of
how the instruments are used and the *voice* of the vocalist may seem
like *little things*, but in God's eyes and ears they are not small. God
did not make them to be used like that.

I hesitate to estimate how times I have heard Christians say: "But
they are using the words of the Bible." I say, "the *sound* contradicts
what is being said," just as much as when a person uses God's name
in vain. We don't commend that person. We say, "Don't use my
Savior's name like that!"

I would like to use one more personal illustration to demonstrate
how much a person's voice has influenced me. One summer I went
to Michigan to study for six weeks with Robert Shaw. It was a real
learning experience for me to work with this great choral conductor
and the visiting experts in that field. However, I drove there and
back in a little VW Beetle that we had at that time.

On my way back home, the engine in that little car broke down
completely so that it could not be fixed, and I was forced to purchase another used Beetle to make the trip the rest of the way home.
Somewhere in North Carolina, I stopped to get something to eat
and decided to call Flora Jean to let her know where I was. As soon
as I heard her voice, I broke down and could not talk because I was
crying so hard. The pressures of the day, having to buy another car
we could not really afford, and wondering how we were going to
survive financially had gotten to me. All it took was the sound of
Flora Jean's voice on that phone to make me realize how much I
needed her and the love she always showed to me.

The book of Psalms refers to the *voice* of the psalmist at least 25 times. Psalm 42:4 mentions "the *voice of joy and praise.*" Hebrews 13:15 admonishes us to "offer the sacrifice of praise to God continually, that is, the fruit of our lips giving thanks to His name." I can't help thinking that the Lord must be pleased when we use the voices He has given us to give praise to Him for all He has done for us. A *little thing* could be a *big thing* for the heart of our Savior who loves us so much.

Chapter 9

How to Resist Temptation

There is nothing wrong in being tempted. We can say that the temptation itself is a *little thing* but the giving in to it is not little. If you are human, you are going to be tempted. People who believe they are sinlessly perfect are sinning against God when they say that because they are lying. There just isn't any such stage for human beings on this earth. You are going to be tempted.

There is nothing wrong with having appetites and desires. There is nothing wrong with getting hungry. God made you with hunger. There's nothing wrong with that. It's the giving in to it such that it becomes too important in your life that is wrong. We must understand that there is going to be temptation in everything that is good if we misuse the desires that God has given us.

The classic Scripture verse that teaches this is 1 Corinthians 10:13. "There hath no temptation taken you but such as is *common to man*: but God is faithful, who will not suffer [allow] you to be tempted above that ye are able; but will with the temptation also make a way to escape, that ye may be able to bear it."

Let's take that verse apart and apply it to each of us.

3. Temptation is "common to man." Your temptation is not unique, no matter what it is. Other people have faced the same kind of temptation and have been able, by God's grace, to get victory over it.

4. "God is faithful!" Victory over temptation is not based on your ability to conquer it. It is based on the *faithfulness* of your Heavenly Father.

5. God will not allow you to be "tempted above that ye are able." None of us can say, "I just couldn't help myself. The temptation was too great." God knows you better than you know yourself, and He will not allow you to have more than you can bear.

6. God *always* makes "a way to escape" from temptation. There is always a way out if we will trust Him to give us the grace. God has not *predestined* us to fail.

7. "That ye may be able to bear it." The load is never too heavy. God's strength is "made perfect in weakness" (2 Cor. 12:9), and He "will supply *all* your need" (Phil. 4:19).

These words from a song I wrote in 1976 relate to this truth.

My grace is sufficient for you,
Forever My promise is true,
Though trials confound you and trouble surrounds you,
My Spirit will make your heart new.
My strength is made perfect in weakness,

My grace will supply all your need,
For all things together work good if you love Me;
My grace is sufficient for you.

Every phrase is from the Bible, and this is one of the few songs I know in which God is speaking to us. "How Firm a Foundation" is another one.

An excellent Bible example of resisting temptation is in Genesis 39 where the young man Joseph resists the beguilement of Potiphar's wife. There are several things that make this temptation extraordinary: Joseph was just a slave; she was the boss's wife; he was prospering in all he did; and it would have been easy for a lesser man to fall for the deceptive idea that no one would ever know. However, the most consequential thing was that if Joseph had not resisted, he never would have ruled Egypt and saved his family when the drought came.

Here is an outline that comes directly from Genesis 39:8-9.

1. He knew how to say NO! "He refused."

2. He valued the trust of others. "My master ... hath committed all that he hath to my hand."

3. He prized his position. "There is none greater in this house than I."

4. He differentiated between what was his and what was not. "Neither hath he kept anything from me *but thee*, because thou art his wife!"

5. He called the temptation by the correct name. "How can I do this *great wickedness*." It was not a *little thing* to Joseph.

6. He brought God into the situation. *"And sin against God."*

There are many other lessons that can be learned from this passage, but I trust this outline will help you meditate on what Joseph did and apply the principles to whatever temptation you are facing.

Chapter 10

A LITTLE DECISION

From the time I was small, I loved music and really enjoyed playing the trombone. My three older siblings played brass instruments, and our parents wanted us to start a brass quartet with two trumpets and two trombones. They somehow found a beat-up old trombone for me and I began to play the trombone at age five.

I played that instrument until age ten when the family wanted to buy a better trombone for my oldest brother, Ed. We all went from door to door in Verona, New Jersey, selling fudge that my grandmother made so that we could buy Ed a new trombone. I then inherited Ed's old trombone where the slide would not stick, and everyone was surprised when I could play the trombone part of marches while listening to a recording of them, never having seen the music. That was no *little thing* for a ten-year-old boy!

I was put in the high school band at age 13, and that same year I won a place in the New Jersey All-State High School Orchestra. I was also a solo artist at the Ocean Grove 10,000-seat auditorium that summer. All through high school I played in marching bands and small symphony orchestras, and I was a guest artist at many places in northern New Jersey and New York.

All of this was overwhelming and breathtaking for a young boy, and I began to feel that I might be "God's gift to the musical world." I will not go into all the things that God allowed to happen to humble me, including having my two front teeth capped. However, when I heard about Bob Jones University through Evangelist Elmer Piper, I found myself on a train to Greenville, South Carolina, in January 1949 with two corduroy jackets, two pairs of corduroy pants, and no idea of how I could go to college with no money.

What was I thinking?! In another chapter I will tell how God got me through school, but for now let me just say that that *little decision* changed my life! Dr. Bob Jones Sr.'s chapel messages spoke to my heart, I loved the rules and regulations, the music was wonderful, and the Bible classes opened my eyes and heart to things I had never seen before.

God got me out of New York where the temptations of the world caught my brother David so that he lost his life at age 28. God protected me and called me into the ministry of music for Him that I have loved and enjoyed for more than 66 years, and best of all, He brought Flora Jean to me so that we could serve Him together all these years.

A little decision? Looking back on it, it may have seemed little, but it was *gigantic*!

Chapter 11

CLOUDS

You may wonder why I am calling clouds just *little things* since they come in all kinds of large and small sizes and shapes in the sky. However, clouds symbolize the *power of God*, and I am including this chapter because clouds are so prevalent that we take them for granted. One of our astronauts commented recently that when he saw a certain hurricane from space, he said it was shaped like a human eye. Clouds are mentioned more than 150 times in Scripture, and so there is no way we can study all of those references in this chapter. However, we can learn a lot about clouds by what Scripture teaches us.

In the Old Testament, there are a number of mentions of clouds that refer to the Shekinah glory of God. The word *Shekinah* does not appear in the Bible, but this special cloud that is the Shekinah signifies the "divine visitation of the presence of God on the earth." The first mention of this is in Exodus 13:20-25. The Lord appeared in a pillar of cloud by day and a pillar of fire by night to guide His people on their way through the wilderness. In Exodus 33, God assured Moses that His presence would be with His people. When the Shekinah glory threw the Egyptian army into confusion in Exodus 14, it was enough to let the Egyptians know that the LORD was fighting against them. Exodus 40:34-38 mentions the cloud five times when Moses and the Israelites set up the tabernacle. This passage calls it "the glory of the LORD" twice and "the cloud of the LORD" once.

My own favorite mention of this singular cloud is in 2 Chronicles 5:11-14 because that passage says that the Shekinah glory (cloud) came as a result of the singers and instruments sounding together praising the Lord as one, saying, "For he is good; for his mercy endureth for ever." That is the "song of the ages." The New Testament puts it another way in Romans 3:26: "To declare ... his righteousness: that he might be just, *and* the justifier of him which believeth in Jesus." God is "just" (always righteous and good), but He can still justify sinners because "his mercy endureth for ever."

As the Israelites were praising God with a fanfare of 120 trumpets (2 Chronicles 5:12), an orchestra of four thousand instruments (1 Chronicles 23:5), and a choir of 80,000 to 200,000 singers (Josephus, Book VII, chapter vii), the temple "was filled with a cloud." That cloud was the Shekinah glory, because the next verse says, "So that the priests could not stand to minister *by reason of the cloud*, for *the glory of the LORD* had filled the house of God."

This was probably some of the most beautiful music that has ever been heard, because 1 Chronicles 25:7 tells us that there were 288 skillful musicians who "were instructed in the songs of the LORD." In other words, these musicians were not thrown together at the last minute for this exciting event of praise to the LORD. A director could not make the enormous group of musicians that were there sing and play together ("as one, to make one sound," v. 13) unless they had practiced and had a skillful conductor.

There are several occasions in the New Testament where the Shekinah glory presence is made known. For instance, Jesus took Peter, James, and John up into a high mountain, the Mount of Transfiguration, where they were to experience a part of His heavenly glory. This was so that the "inner circle" of His disciples could gain a greater understanding of who Jesus was. Christ underwent a dramatic change in appearance in order that the disciples could behold Him in His glory (the Shekinah cloud). That experience was no small thing. The disciples, who had known Him only in His human body, now had a greater realization of the deity of Christ, though they could not fully comprehend it. That realization gave them the reassurance they needed after hearing the shocking news of His coming death.

Notice how verse 5 describes the experience: "Behold, a bright cloud overshadowed them: and a voice out of the cloud, which said, 'This is my beloved Son in whom I am well pleased; hear ye Him.'" But also notice verse 6: "And when the disciples heard it, they fell on their face, and were sore afraid." This is what always happens when mere men meet God or are in His presence; they don't brag about it but fall flat on their faces!

This is the same thing as when Isaiah met the Shekinah glory in Isaiah 6. When the voice that spoke cried, "Holy, holy, holy," "the posts of the door moved at the *voice* of him that cried, and the house was filled with smoke" (a cloud, the Shekinah glory). Watch Isaiah's response: "Woe is me! For I am undone!" I like the way the Spanish Bible translates Isaiah's response: "¡Ay de mi! que soy muerto!" ("I am dead!) In other words, why am I still breathing? I have seen the presence of God.

The book of Revelation has three references to clouds: 10:1, 11:12, and 14:14-16, where a cloud is mentioned four times. The reference in 10:1 appears to be the Shekinah glory when it says, "And I saw another mighty angel come down from heaven, *clothed with a cloud*: and a rainbow was on his head, and his face were as it was the sun, and his feet as pillars of fire."

There is not enough room in this book to write about all the Bible says about clouds. I hope someone reading this will further study clouds and their power.

Chapter 12

✦

THE POWER OF GOD

I mentioned in Chapter 11 that clouds symbolize the power of God. Anyone who has ever flown an airplane, and particularly a small airplane, knows that clouds have power. Cumulonimbus clouds (white fluffy clouds that are dense and vertically developed) may look beautiful on the outside, but they can be devastatingly dangerous on the inside, and they are not a *little thing*, especially to the pilot of a small airplane.

My father got his "wings" in the First World War and taught airmen to fly high-powered airplanes in the Second World War, so I guess I inherited his love for flying. I didn't learn to fly until I was 43 years old, but in the 18 years that I logged 3500 hours as a pilot in small airplanes, I learned to respect clouds. Flying a small airplane is "hours upon hours of boredom, punctuated by moments of sheer terror," and I have experienced both. Many of the "sheer terror" moments come as a result of getting into or too close to powerful clouds.

Let me relate one incident that will demonstrate what I just wrote. My son Randy and I left Denver, Colorado, on May 17, 1978, headed toward Phoenix, Arizona, in the Piper Seneca airplane (PA-34) that we owned at that time. The Denver flight control had told me that there were clouds directly west of Denver, and they suggested that I deviate south to Colorado Springs before heading west.

We were at about 8,000 feet at Colorado Springs when we turned west to head toward the Ute Pass where 12,000 feet of altitude would get us through safely. Shortly after leaving Colorado Springs, we saw what looked like a small cloud in the shape of a hammock directly in front of us. Since we were climbing at about 200 feet a minute, I calculated that we could climb right over the "hammock" without any trouble. What a mistake!

The cloud was "climbing" faster than we were so that as we got over it, it caught us and started lifting us at 1,000 feet per minute. There was no way of controlling the airplane. The cloud was tossing us around, things were flying around inside the airplane, the windows were icing up, and we were at the mercy of the cloud. I remember saying to Randy: "We had better pray!" I thought that because there was an updraft lifting us, there would be a downdraft on the other side ahead of us that would pull us down into the cliffs below us.

I don't know how long this terrifying event lasted—it seemed like hours—but it must have been about 15 minutes, estimating that we were around 10,000 feet when we went in and that the cloud spit us out at 26,000 feet. Fortunately, that airplane had oxygen bottles, but it was the protection of the Lord that kept us alive; and we landed safely in Phoenix to minister there.

If you would like to read about another aircraft incident I experienced, look up pages 105-107 in *I Being in the Way, the Lord Led Me*, my autobiography written in 2010. Thunderclouds were involved in that one. I was at the Flushing Airport near LaGuardia Airport, and thunderstorms kept me on the runway for several hours before I could take off. I was then vectored around storms on my way to Atlantic City, New Jersey. Because those same storms had left a lot of water on the runway at Bader Field there when I landed, the airplane was hydroplaning and I went into the water at the end of the runway. The water was only up to the wings, but *The Atlantic City Tribune* highlighted their article about my adventure with the headline: Music in the "oops" Air!

Chapter 13

"Take No Thought"

You may wonder why "taking no thought" would be in *Little Things*. Let me explain at the outset of this chapter. These *little things* of life are things or events that happen when you are least expecting them, and your response at those times is *not* a *little thing*. It can mean the difference between success and failure, or it might even be a life-changing experience!

In the first three Gospel accounts, Matthew, Mark, and Luke, it is recorded that Jesus told the disciples to "take no thought" about what they were to say when they were brought before governors and kings for His sake (Matthew 10:18). In verse 19, he said, "For it shall be given you in that same hour what ye shall speak." In verse 20, the Lord goes even further to tell them: "For it is not ye that speak, but the Spirit of your Father which speaketh in you."

Mark approaches Christ's answer a little differently and adds that Christ said they should not even "premeditate" about what they might want to say when they were being challenged (Mark 13:11). Luke, who always seemed to remember lots of details, mentions several groups who were going to make the disciples look foolish as they appeared before them (Luke 12:11).

There seems to be some confusion in Bible commentaries about how Christ was instructing the disciples concerning what they were to do in those situations. Some people, including some I have come across in my Pentecostal background, have thought that "Bible education" was not necessary since the Holy Spirit would guide you whenever you were speaking for the Lord. I have known some who have even thought that Bible training was a waste of valuable time and that because of the "urgency of the hour" they must get the message out *now*!

One commentary says that since the disciples were basically "unlearned men," they would be overwhelmed and intimidated by the scholars, the governors, and the kings of their day. Therefore, they should not try to persuade those who were interrogating them.

Another commentary comes closer to the truth by saying that since in the final analysis we always have to depend on the Holy Spirit to guide us and since He will be "effectual" in bringing about the desired result, preparation is not necessary. Some songwriters and hymn writers have used that thinking to justify sloppy work and poor writing when they actually did not have the proper preparation.

Still another commentary implies that since the Lord is referring to persecution, their suffering or martyrdom will speak loudly enough that they do not need to say anything. However, history tells of many who have loudly proclaimed how thankful they were to be suffering for the Lord, some who were even being burned at the stake for their Savior. I like what a country preacher once had to say about this: "The Bible sure does shed a lot of light on them commentaries."

I believe Christ, with His foreknowledge and unlimited foresight into the future, was able to see into the times when His disciples would be confronted by skeptics and situations for which there is no possibility of preparing. I will talk about some that I personally have experienced in the next chapter. They may have seemed like *little things* at the time, but they definitely were not.

Chapter 14

UNWANTED SURPRISES

When I began a ministry of showing what was happening with music and how it was affecting society in general and churches in particular, I asked the Lord for two specific things. Since I knew I was going to be in a battle against the devil and the world, I first asked the Lord to keep me sweet in the battle and not get bitter. I think the Lord helped me with that and His help guided me in many situations.

The second thing I asked the Lord for was to keep me from getting caught by the very thing I was fighting. I know preachers who became so involved in fighting evil that they were caught by the evil they were fighting. That was true of one evangelist for whom I led singing at youth rallies when I was a teenager. He fought pornography so much that he was caught by it. We fight evil, but we don't want to focus on it so much that it captures us as well.

I want to mention just two events of my ministry that started out as *little things* and ended up, at least in my mind, as *big things. There was no way I could have prepared for what was coming!* Many years ago, sometime before 1973, I was invited to speak at a church and youth rally in Dallas, Texas. On the Monday after the rally and the church service on Sunday, the pastor of the church arranged for me to be interviewed about rock music on a Christian radio station in Dallas on Monday. I should have known there was trouble ahead when I saw that the station was called "The Station of *Love*."

When the pastor dropped me off at the station, I was told by the secretary that I was not to be interviewed. The station manager had read my book, *The Big Beat*, the night before, and he had decided it was going to be a debate between him and me on the air that day. I was to be on the air answering questions from him and listeners for half an hour. I said OK, thinking I could probably handle being challenged with things I had already faced. There was no way I could know what was coming!

There was a long table in the studio with him at one end and me at the other end, with one of their employees as a "moderator" on one side between us. They began the program with some "Christian" rock music and asked me to comment on it. I proceeded to explain why it was bad music: too much rhythm, too loud and raucous, accents in the wrong places, constant repetition, etc. They then said, "We have the composer of this music on the phone, he's been listening to you, and we want you to talk to him." Nice, agreeable, congenial, and easy to get along with people!?

I don't remember the composer's last name, but I know his first name was Rick. I immediately addressed him and went over again on the air what I had just said. After a couple of minutes back and forth, the Lord just seemed to say (not in an audible voice, but it certainly was strong to me) *ask him about his salvation*. I hesitated a little until the urge became stronger. So I said, "Rick, tell me about your salvation!" He hemmed and hawed before he said, "I was at Explo 72, and the music was so strong, I had to make a decision." By the way, Explo 72 was where Kris Kristofferson was featured. He is the same performer who said, "They accuse me of being on a Jesus trip; they refuse to see that I'm *just being humorous.*"

I then said, "Rick, what Scripture brought you to Christ?" When he had no reply, I gave him a short synopsis of the plan of salvation. He had no idea what I was talking about. And then, with Rick still on the phone listening, I said to the two men sitting at the table: "Gentlemen, it's obvious we are talking to an unsaved man." They had no answer.

They quickly got Rick off the phone, and for the next hour and a half, with many listeners calling in, proceeded to question me. One of their first arguments was this: "Where does the Bible say 'thou shalt not use rock?'" To that I said, "Gentlemen, let's be reasonable. There are many things the Bible doesn't mention specifically, but it does give us Christian principles by which we live. For instance, 1 Corinthians 3:16 says that our bodies are the 'temple of the Holy Spirit.' God lives in us, and that is why we don't drink alcohol or smoke." I found out later that the station manager had a pack of cigarettes in his pocket right there in the studio!

The "interview" and questions from their listeners went on for over two hours that morning. I must admit that I was very aware that God was directing me in that situation, because there was no way I could have adequately prepared for it. But let me give you the clincher. This was a station that used advertising, and when the three of us went out into the lobby as I was about to leave, one of their most prominent advertisers was there. He looked at those two men, and pointing to me, said, "You gentlemen need to listen to this man. *He is telling you the truth!*"

On another occasion, I was invited to speak at a youth rally in Jacksonville, North Carolina. There was a group of about 35 to 40 hippies at the meeting, and after the meeting they invited me to go to their "pad" so that they could ask questions. I was there until about 2 a.m. being peppered with all kinds of questions, and this was another opportunity for me to give a presentation of the gospel. Although none of them made a decision that I know of that night, I remember what they said: "We disagree with you, but we appreciate your being so nice to us and listening to our questions." I did the *little thing* that God wanted me to do, and as always, the results are in His hands.

(See Chapter 52 of this book for another event that involved hippies.)

Chapter 15

🐦

FATHER AND MOTHER

It is amazing how many times the Bible mentions something and seems to treat it as a *little thing* when it actually is a *big thing*. Perhaps the problem is not with the Bible but with us as readers of the Bible. We take too many things for granted, often because we are so familiar with them.

The word "father" is mentioned 979 times in the Bible, and the word "mother" is mentioned 244 times. The reason that God, who is *the Master Communicator*, refers to fathers and mothers so often is that He wants us to know how important they both are to us as His children.

We will refer to God as our Father later in this chapter, but the fact that Joseph's father, Jacob, is mentioned almost 50 times in the last section of the book of Genesis makes it stand out as something significant. Many of these times are when Joseph asks his brothers about the welfare of their (and his) father. The sin and the guilty consciences of those men kept them from understanding why this powerful man wanted to know about their father.

However, we must not miss the fact that Joseph, the youngest of the brothers at that time, witnessed the death of his real mother, Rachel, as she gave birth to Benjamin on the way to Canaan as the family fled from Haran. Joseph must have gone through "the valley of sorrow" when he lost his mother as a young boy. The softness and sensitivity he shows later on gives insight into the relationship he must have had with his mother.

Although the Bible nowhere asserts that Joseph was a type of Christ, there are at least twenty things that demonstrate that possibility. His love for his father is one of the main ways that we can see that typology illustrated.

That brings us to the relationship between Jesus and *His* Father. In the book of John alone, we read that Jesus mentioned His Father at least 196 times, and many of those times He called God "my Father." I believe this is one of the reasons that Jerome Hines, the great opera singer, is one of the many who found Christ by reading and believing the book of John. The Scripture reveals an intimate, personal, one-on-one communion between the Lord Jesus Christ and God the Father. As he said, "I and the Father are one."

This also opens one of the names that the Bible uses for God, and this name is another *little thing* that is actually a *big thing*. Since both the Father and the Son are God, this name intrinsically refers to both of them. That name is *El Shaddai*. Investigation into the derivation of that name is both interesting and touching since it seems to imply that our God acts as both Father and Mother to His children.

Now, we are not saying that God is both male and female. However, when we read that God is our "Shepherd," that is a metaphor to reveal how God takes care of us. When Psalm 91 says that God "covers us with His feathers," and "under His wings we trust," He is using the metaphor of a bird to reveal part of His character. By the same token, when we look at the name *El Shaddai*, it reveals a metaphor that shows that God can act as both Father and Mother for those who trust Him.

El is the Hebrew word for "The Strong One" as in Genesis 1:1, where we read, "In the beginning God [Elohim] created." *Elohim* is a plural-form name that signifies that our God is strong and that He is Three in One. That name is called a "uni-plurality" and is the first indication in the Bible that God is a Trinity.

In the compound name "El Shaddai," the Hebrew word that modifies *El* is *Shad*, and that Hebrew word is always used in Scripture for a woman's breast, particularly a mother's. The best place in Scripture where *El Shaddai* is used will illustrate this point. Genesis 17:1 tells how the Lord appeared to Abram (as his name was called at that point) and said, "I am *El Shaddai*." That is when God changed Abram's name to Abraham, when he was 99. He changed Sarai's name to Sarah when she was 90.

The next thing that happens is when Abraham and Sarah learn they are going to have a baby although they are "old and well stricken in age." Sarah laughs because she can't believe it. Through the name *El Shaddai*, God is telling them that He is the "All-Sufficient One" and nothing is too hard for Him (Genesis 18:14). Notice that this was for *both* Abraham (father) and Sarah (mother) that God was nourishing them as a mother strengthens her child from her own body. That was a *little thing* that became a *big thing* for Abraham and Sarah—to become a father and mother at their ripe old age.

A further study of this name is illuminating for anyone who wants to understand this aspect of God's wonderful almighty character. The KJV invariably uses the word "Almighty" in the Old Testament when the Hebrew is *El Shaddai* (Gen. 17:1; 28:3; 35:11; 43:14; 48:3; 49:24-25; and Ps. 91:1). The word *Shaddai* by itself is used 48 times in Scripture.

Since this word is used so often in speaking to fathers, we would not be wrong in showing this name for God as particularly relating to them: Abraham, when God gave him the Abrahamic Covenant in Genesis 17:1; Jacob, when Isaac and Rebekah sent him to the house of Bethuel in Genesis 28:3 and at Bethel in 35:11; and Joseph's brothers, when Jacob finally allows them to take Benjamin down to Egypt in Genesis 43:14. This name also occurs thirty-one times in the book of Job, particularly where God is answering Job at the end of the book about him (Job 40:2). Then, a little later in Job 42:12-13, we read:

> So the LORD blessed the latter end of Job more than his beginning: for he had fourteen thousand sheep, and six thousand camels, and a thousand yoke of oxen, and a thousand she asses. He also had seven sons and three daughters.

El Shaddai blessed Job as a father!

Chapter 16

NO DOUBT!

I should say at the beginning of this chapter that I have *absolutely no doubt* that God had me be born to the right parents at the right time. He also gave me the right family that He wanted me to have. As I look back on those early years of my life, I can see that the Lord was orchestrating every facet of those experiences to prepare me for the things that he had planned for me. They may have been *little things* at the time, but looking back at them, they were substantial.

Edward Arthur Garlock, my Dad, was taken out of school after the seventh grade to meet the needs of his family. He joined the Air Corps when he was seventeen, and that is when he learned to fly a plane. When his oldest brother, Henry (author of *Before We Kill and Eat You*), was called to preach and became a missionary to Africa, Dad thought he needed to become a preacher too, so he went to Bible school.

However, Dad was not really cut out to be a preacher. In fact, Dad did not get a high school education, but he loved math, electricity, and aviation and got a degree in those three subjects by correspondence later in his life. He had a brilliant mind and could repair anything, so he became a mechanic who could fix speedometers, starters, generators, and many other things. During World War II, Dad even taught radial engines, theory of flight, and so on at the Casey Jones School of Aeronautics in Newark, New Jersey, and at LaGuardia Airport in New York. He was also a test pilot for some very fast airplanes, one of which was called the Brewster.

Dad must have been an excellent pilot, because some of the fighter pilots that he taught to fly in the Brewster called it "a flying coffin." However, Dad could not only fly that plane, but he could teach others to fly it as well. By following my Dad's instructions, they learned to be fighter pilots. I don't think we kids ever realized how talented and brilliant our father was.

If my father were alive today, he would probably say I was making something big out of something small. But as I look back on how humble and unassuming my dad was, I was instinctively learning things from him.

Here are just a few of the things I was learning: how to work hard; how to be unselfish; how to pay attention to details; how to love my wife; how to give my best; how to *not* let being poor keep me from accomplishing something; how to love all my children equally; how to always be cheerful; and more. I could give an illustration for every one of those character traits, but I think you have probably gotten the idea of what kind of man my father was.

Mom was the "queen bee" of our house. She had only one brother, and he died of leukemia when he was 21. My mother's father was a good businessman, so although he was not rich, they always had nice things as she was growing up. I am sure Mom had to make many adjustments in trying to take care of the many children she wanted to have, and she always stretched what little money we had to do the best she could for each one of us nine children.

For instance, when Christmas rolled around and there was little money to buy very much, we each had a "pile" under the Christmas tree with whatever she could scrape together. Mom had a big heart, and each one of us knew she loved us with all of that big heart.

Mom was also very talented, and she could improvise almost any song on the piano and play it in any key that would fit a particular vocalist or instrumentalist. One of the best things Mom did for me was the hours she spent playing the piano along with me on the trombone as I was learning to improvise. She and I spent many hours together. I believe those hours with her helped me develop feeling, phrasing, tone color, variety, melodic line, and tone-painting of the words of the song, and just plain enjoying the music we were playing together.

One of Mom's best qualities was her ability to be an encourager. She was the one who first told me that she thought I had a beautiful tone on the trombone. Her comments made me want to work on it to make it better. She also appreciated anything I did around the house to help her keep things clean. She always said, "We may be poor, but we can be clean." And she encouraged me in that area as well. She said, "If you want it done right, get Frank to do it!"

I would not trade anything for all the things I learned from my parents that have kept me going for the last 70 years or so since I left home to go to Bob Jones University and learn to serve the Lord.

The discipline I learned at home made it easy for me to adjust to the rules at BJU and to the stresses that come with ministry. I suppose the best thing of all that I learned was to love the Lord with all my heart and to give my best to Him.

Many, many thanks, Dad and Mom!

Chapter 17

[hummingbird ornament]

FOR JUST A LITTLE TIME

The title for this chapter comes from a word that we do not use very much today. Perhaps we should, however, because we often do what the word means without realizing it. The word is *sojourn*, which actually means "to stay in a place for a little time."

The first instance of this in the Bible is when there was a famine in the land of Canaan and Abram left the land he was promised by God and went to Egypt to "sojourn" (Genesis 12:10). This was the time that Abram left the place of blessing (Canaan) and got into trouble (in Egypt) because he did not trust God.

The second instance is when two angels came to visit Lot in wicked Sodom where he came to "sojourn" (Genesis 19:9). If the angels had not delivered him, Lot and his family would have lost everything that night. It is also revealing to note that when there was another famine in Canaan, God told Isaac not to go down to Egypt, but to stay in Canaan. Isaac in this case did the same thing that Abram had done and did not trust God, but out of fear he told the people of Gerar that Rebekah was his sister (Genesis 26:3).

There is one mention of "sojourning" in the book of Judges (17:8-9) when "every man did that which was right in his own eyes" (17:6). This was another occasion of civil and religious disobedience.

The classic instance of the problem of "sojourning" and thinking it is a *little thing* is in the book of Ruth, just after the book of Judges. This is a different case where a famine caused a family to leave Bethlehem-Judah, "the house of bread and praise," and to go to *sojourn* in Moab (the place of disobedience, defeat and disgrace).

In other words, Elimelech, whose name means "God is my King," leaves the place of God's will to *sojourn* in the place of self-desire and continues there longer than he expected. In fact, it was longer than he could have imagined since he lost his life and the lives of his two sons there as well. He did not intend to stay. He thought it would be just to *sojourn* for a little time. What he thought was just *a small decision* that would not have any consequences turned out to be *a major decision* that affected not only him, but his whole family.

The best principle the Bible gives us in this regard is Proverbs 3:5-6, which are Flora Jean's life verses:

> *Trust in the LORD with all thine heart, and lean not unto thine own understanding. In all thy ways acknowledge him, and he shall direct thy paths.*

We never know when a small decision might be one that will bring about important results in the future. That is why we must commit our lives to God every day of our lives and ask Him to give us wisdom in every decision we make (James 1:5).

If any of you lack wisdom, let him ask of God, that giveth to all men liberally, and upbraideth not; and it shall be given him.

Chapter 18

A Leap of Faith

I must begin this chapter with a confession: I regretfully admit that I have not always followed the Lord as I should have. I know I was saved when my grandmother led me to the Lord at age five. However, there were many times when I followed some little things like the example of Elimelech (not knowing I was doing it). I could make all kinds of excuses for my lack of trust, but none of them really excuse me.

I always knew down in my heart that God loved me and that I wanted to serve Him some day. But as with Elimelech, the spiritual famine in which I often found myself influenced me so that I was not all that God wanted me to be. Part of this thinking related to the inconsistencies that I saw in the Pentecostal churches my parents sometimes attended. However, I know I should have been looking to the Lord instead of those around me.

I suppose my weakest time was during my teenage years. I wanted to be popular. The things of the world, especially in the area of music, had a tremendous allure for me. In high school, the administration always had me read the Scripture and pray in the general assemblies of the student body because they knew I planned to be a preacher.

However, I also played in a dance band and was a part of many programs and shows that I had no business being in. I would play for a dance on Saturday evening and ride my bike three miles to play in the Caldwell Baptist Church on Sunday morning.

In a way, I guess I was sojourning in Moab during those years. At age 15, my two older brothers and I formed a trio that had a ministry in many churches all over New England. We also played and sang at the Word of Life Rallies and The Bowery Mission in downtown New York. Meanwhile, I was still in the dance band. I was a lukewarm Christian at best, and that is what Moab represents in the Bible.

When I was 17, Phil Saint, a gospel chalk artist, invited me to work with him and lead the singing in his meetings. I also helped package and ship out his well-known painting, "The Way of the Cross," that sold over 50,000 prints. I thoroughly enjoyed leading singing for Phil, and I should have realized that the Lord might be calling me to a music ministry, but I did not. I guess I was afraid He might ask me to do something I didn't want to do.

That is why I am still amazed that at age 18, two weeks after hearing about Bob Jones University, I found myself on the Silver Meteor train as a passenger on my way to Greenville, South Carolina. This was a leap of faith for me as I had never been farther south than Delaware and the South was a "strange country" to this New Jersey boy.

I remember thinking on that trip: "What am I doing? I have no money. I have only two pair of corduroy pants and two corduroy jackets. What led me to say, "Yes. I will go to a 'strange country,' not knowing what lies ahead"?

Looking back, I can see that God was in that seemingly small decision. It really was a *big* one! Had I not gone to Greenville in God's will, I could easily have gotten mixed up in the worldly music culture in New York; I never would have found God's will for my life; I never would have met Flora Jean, my wonderful, musical life partner and companion for all these years; and I would have missed all the wonderful opportunities that the Lord has given me to serve Him. That was no "little decision." It was a life-changing one that set the course for me that I have followed for the past 70 years.

If you would like to read further about how God has led me, I have written two books that will fill in many of the details: *I Being in the Way, the Lord Led Me* and *Just Show Up: God Can Use You.* The first one tells of the many miracles that God has wrought for me, and the second one tells how I "just showed up." When I did, God used that to give me the opportunity to use my spiritual gift of encouraging others to use their God-given talents in serving Him.

Chapter 19

A CLINGING VINE

Two chapters ago, we saw that a small decision like sojourning can actually be a life-changing decision that one is not aware of at the time. That was true of Elimelech and his family who left "the house of bread and praise" because there was famine there. In this chapter, we will look at a good decision that was recorded in the same chapter of the Bible as Elimelech's wrong decision. That decision was made by a young girl who, according to her background, had no basis on which to make such a consequential decision that would not only affect her, but put her in the "generation of Jesus Christ" (Matthew 1:5).

In contrast to Elimelech, who thought his decision was only going to be a sojourn in Moab, Ruth's decision to go with Naomi was intended as a permanent one. That decision would bring her to Bethlehem-Judah, "the house of bread and praise," the place that Elimelech left because there was a famine.

It is also important for us to notice that there was no way Ruth could possibly have even considered that her vow would be recorded, memorized, studied, analyzed, and written about for more than three thousand years after she made it. However, that is the way God often works. He takes what might seem to be a little decision by a young widow and turns it into a monumental standard for others to follow for so many years.

There is an important principle that applies to Ruth and many other characters in the Bible. It also applies to us now—whenever a person follows whatever light God has shown him or her, God will then reveal the next step to be taken. So often, we want God to reveal the next step before we take the one He has shown. He does not work that way! Think of how little light Ruth must have received from her backslidden family to make the commitment she does in Ruth 1:16-17. Do we think any member of Elimelech's family told her how wonderful it was to serve God?

There are so many salient aspects to this story that we will not be able to explore all of them. However, we will look at several. The first aspect we notice is that Naomi, Ruth's mother-in-law, tried to discourage her. In fact, she actually gives Ruth at least a dozen reasons (Ruth 1:11-13) why she should not go to Bethlehem-Judah with her. Even those reasons do not take into account that Naomi might be embarrassed to bring a Moabite girl back home with her to show her friends.

I do not have the answer for the important question of what was working in the heart and mind of Ruth for her to make a statement that we might expect of a mature Christian girl who had known the Lord for a long time. Where did she develop that sterling character that she demonstrates, such that she has a whole book of the Bible named after her?

That being said, let's look at what Ruth said to her mother-in-law, which has been repeated in weddings all over the world for centuries. The first thing I want us to notice is Ruth's **Commitment**: "Whither thou goest, I will go." That's why this chapter is called "a clinging vine." Ruth would not take "no" for an answer. There was no turning back in her mind. Remember that her Moabite background was a place where God was not worshipped and people did whatever seemed good to them. Not Ruth!

The second thing is her **Contentment**: "Where thou lodgest, I will lodge." This gives up all freedom! She is saying, "I will be content to live wherever you live." (A tent or a cottage, why should I care.) At the time she said this, Naomi had nothing to offer her. For all she knew, there was no "home" back in Bethlehem-Judah.

The third thing is **Communion**: "Thy people shall be my people." She was not only saying she would love Naomi's family. She was saying she would love God's people. When you come to God, you get His people too. That is where your fellowship and communion ought to be. God's people are not of this world. Ruth was completely forsaking all the family and relatives she had in Moab to have communion with people who love God. Yet today many people who say they are Christians never attend any church.

The fourth thing is **Confession**: "Thy God [shall be] my God." Notice how the steps get stronger each time. Ruth promises to give up her Moabite gods and worship with Naomi. Ruth turned to God from idols just as 1 Thessalonians 1:9 says of Christians. This was a giant step of faith for Ruth. Her eternal destiny was at stake.

The fifth thing is **Continuation**: "Where thou diest, will I die." This is a decision that is never to be reversed or altered. It is permanent. Ruth set her face steadfastly towards Bethlehem-Judah. She was additionally promising to be with Naomi in her old age. She promised to love her mother-in-law unconditionally until the end, whenever that might be.

The sixth thing is **Completion**: "There will I be buried." Ruth did not even want her mortal remains to go back to Moab. Love has reached its highest peak and abandonment here. She wanted even the remains of her body to be in God's territory, the Promised Land. Ruth wanted to be buried in Bethlehem-Judah.

The seventh and last thing has two aspects: **Contemplation** and **Consecration**: "The LORD do so to me, and more also, if ought but death part thee and me." Why does it matter where one is buried? Ruth is a girl who has tremendous faith in God. She evidently must have heard about and believed in the resurrection.

Elimelech and Naomi, even though they were not where God wanted them to be, must have told Ruth and Orpah some of the Jewish sayings and proverbs like the one Ruth quotes here. It is as if she says, "May the Lord's severest punishment come upon me if I do not do what I promise."

This is why I have called number seven Contemplation and Consecration. She may have been contemplating the resurrection just as Abraham, Isaac, Jacob, and Joseph had likely done in wanting to all be in the Promised Land when the Resurrection occurs. In Hebrews 11:17-19 we see Abraham's belief in resurrection:

*By faith, Abraham, when he was tried, offered up Isaac; and he that had received the promises offered up his only begotten son ... Accounting that **God was able to raise him up**, even from the dead; from whence also he received him in a figure."*

What we have just studied is probably the best statement of consecration that can be found anywhere. It is particularly noteworthy in that it is a daughter-in-law speaking to her mother-in-law and not the other way around. It is also remarkable in that it comes from a Moabite girl who had married into an Israelite family, had lost her husband, had only heard about God from weak believers, and who promises to go to a country she has never seen.

The similarities between Ruth and Abraham, who were separated by about 800 years, are astounding. Compare what we have just studied with Genesis 12:1:

Now the LORD had said unto Abram, Get thee out of thy country, and from thy kindred, and from thy father's house, unto a land that I will show thee."

God must have also spoken to Ruth for her to make such a promise to her mother-in-law. She was not only "a clinging vine," she became *a part of the vine itself.* As the Lord Jesus Christ said in John 15:5:

I am the vine, ye are the branches: He that abideth in me, and I in him, the same bringeth forth much fruit; for without me ye can do nothing."

He also said,

Before Abraham was, I Am.

We must remember that Christ, who is the same "yesterday, today, and forever" (Hebrews 13:8), was God in Ruth's day too. And she, like other Old Testament saints, was evidently looking forward by faith to His coming the first time, and to the resurrection at His Second Coming when all Christians will go to be with Him forever.

We definitely cannot say that Ruth knew all this that day. It had to be her simple trust in God at that point that gave her the insight and the confidence to believe what little she knew about the ways of God to completely commit herself to His care. May we all trust God just as Ruth did!

Chapter 20

My Calling

Some of you reading this may have read my autobiography, *I Being in the Way, the Lord Led Me.* If you have, you might remember how I was able to go to Bob Jones University through the generosity of Mrs. Elma Cook. She was the kind woman who paid my way for the three and a half years I studied at BJU.

In the back of that book, in Appendix B, is the story of her husband, Charles, who became a wealthy man although he was "A Genius Who Never Walked a Step." His inventions were used in many places including steam-powered ships in World War I. Some of the money he made in the late 19th century and early 20th century was what his nurse who became his wife used to put me through college after he died.

However, Mrs. Cook had it in her mind that, perhaps because my grandmother told her I wanted to serve the Lord, I had to become a pastor after I graduated. A problem arose for me during my time at BJU in that I realized, from studying music in the Bible, that there were full-fledged priests in the Bible whose ministry was nothing more than music.

*And these were the singers, chief of the fathers of the Levites, who remaining in the chambers were free; for they were employed **in that work day and night*** (1 Chronicles 9:33).

Through that and other passages of His Word, God was indicating to me that I had to make a decision that I do not think Mrs. Cook fully understood. Was I to do what she wanted me to do since she had financed my education, or was I to do what I felt very strongly the Lord wanted me to do?

Now, at this point, I should say that by the grace of God I have probably preached more than many pastors. There have been many, many weeks in which I have preached at least somewhere between 15 and 20 times that week. Not many pastors have done that, and that was done on and off for the almost 70 years that I had a very active ministry in over 50 countries. I have recently held full seminars in Nicaragua, Mexico, Haiti, and Honduras since I turned 80, preaching many times in each country.

Be that as it may, although I still love to teach and preach the Bible, the major part of my ministry through all these years was in the field of music. In fact, my being in that field has opened doors for me that never would have opened if I had been only a preacher. In the early years, my speaking about Biblical principles of music to large groups gave opportunities for me to give the gospel to many people who came to hear me as a musician and then trusted Christ as I wove the gospel into my messages.

Since I was one of the first classically trained musicians to take a stand for the principles of music that were being violated in the secular realm and then in the sacred field, I had opportunities that I never would have had as a preacher. God did not make a mistake when He called me into the field of music, both sacred and secular.

As a young person, I erroneously thought that if a person wanted to serve the Lord, he had to do something that would make him miserable. I envisioned jungles and diseases and all kinds of hardships. God has allowed me to serve Him with something that I love and enjoy. Composing music is hard work, but I enjoy the work! Memorizing operas is long hours of strenuous work, but I have enjoyed conducting ten operas from memory. I should also say that I really do not "memorize" the operas: I *live* them as I conduct them. I become a part of the action!

However, my greatest joy is doing music that is a blessing and encouragement to other people. Just last week, a friend said this to me: "When I read or sing your songs, *I see your heart.*" I thanked him profusely for one of the best things anyone could ever say to me. I *do* want people to see my heart. I have made many mistakes, but I believe God has overridden those mistakes because He knows my heart.

In one of the songs I have written, there is this line from my heart:

> *Lord Jesus, although my flesh is weak,*
> *Lord Jesus, it is Thy will I seek.*

Tonight, at the church where I now attend and still play my trombone, a friend came up to where I was before the service and said, "Not many directors do what you have always done: have us sing the words and lead them in a way that points to the message of what you are leading." Again, I sincerely thanked my friend for recognizing what I have always tried to do in leading a choir or a congregation in singing.

I mention all this to say that I am so glad God called me to do something for Him through music. Music is like nothing else in allowing me to serve my Savior, whom I love with all my heart. I believe Mrs. Cook, who is now in heaven, realizes that she did not make a mistake in paying my way through college so that I could serve the Lord though music more effectively than any other way.

Chapter 21

WHAT'S IN A NAME

Most people never stop to think about the meaning of their name, but that was not always the case. In fact, names in the Bible were not *little things* because they almost always had meanings attached to them. It is almost unbelievable that God (Genesis 2:19-20) let Adam name all the animals: "every beast of the field, and every fowl of the air." That appears to indicate that Adam must have been involved in a highly intellectual and meaningful activity when he gave names to each kind of animal and bird. What a monumental task!

Names were important to Joseph. When he had become a ruler, he let the Egyptians know that he remembered his heritage by the names he gave his two sons when they were born. The first one he called Manasseh, which means "forgetful," because he said that God had allowed him to forget all his toil and all his father's house. The second son he called Ephraim, which means "fruitful," because he said that God had made him "fruitful in the land of my affliction."

One of the most significant characteristics of our omniscient God in giving names is that He not only "tells the number of the stars in the universe," He also *"calls them all by their names"* and that is not a *little thing* (Psalm 147:4; Isaiah 40:26). On the surface, that may not mean much to us. However, the Hebrew word for assigning a name (*shem*) to something is momentous. It is not a meaningless designation; it involves an understanding of the basic characteristics and attributes of the object being named. That means God bestowed individual characteristics on each star and named each one of the billions of stars according to its singular attributes!

There are many times where God also changed the names of *people* for a very specific reason. When God made a covenant with Abraham and made His promise to him, He changed his name from Abram to Abraham. Abram means "noble father" but he becomes Abraham the "father of many." God also changed Sarai, "princess" to Sarah the "mother of nations" (Genesis 17:5, 16). That signifies that the names they were called by God were important to Him.

At the same time (Genesis 18) God revealed Himself by a name that must have been unknown before this, because this is the first mention of that specific name in the Bible. That name was *El Shaddai*. God was showing them that He was to be to them the "All-Sufficient One" who would give Abraham the ability to father a son at 99 years of age and Sarah to become a mother at 90 years of age. There is no way this could be called a *little* thing.

By the way, both Abraham and Sarah laughed when they realized what God was telling them (Genesis 17:17; 18:12). Every name that God calls Himself and that the Bible uses for our Heavenly Father reveals something about the character and greatness of our Omnipotent God. As the Lord Himself said to Abraham:

Is any thing too hard for the LORD?

It is not a joke to God when He makes His promises. All of these things were evidently big to God. *El Shaddai* is one of those special names that demonstrates God's power.

Another instance of God's changing a person's name was at Penuel ("the face of God") where Jacob "wrestled" with God and had his name changed from Jacob ("supplanter") to Israel ("a prince with God"). God appears to want the name of the person to match what He desires that person to be.

Other names reveal a lot about a person, an occasion, or an event. A few examples are Babel (Genesis 11:9), "confusion"; Jehoval-jireh (Genesis 22:14), "Jehovah will see to it"; Moses (Exodus 2:10), "to draw out" (because Pharaoh's daughter "drew him out of the water"); Mount Sinai (Exodus 19), "Mountain of Divine Truth"; Jerusalem, "City of Peace"; Atonement (Hebrew *kaphar*), "to cover"; Redeemer (Hebrew *goel*), "the One who pays;" Aaron, "set apart"; and Joshua (Hebrew *Je-hoshua*), "Jehovah-Savior."

In the next chapter, I will talk about my name. Perhaps I can encourage my readers to find out the meanings of their names as well.

Chapter 22

>

GOD'S PRESENCE

Overemphasizing anything can turn it into a bad thing, and that is what I want to avoid in this chapter. If we put too much emphasis on names and their meanings, we become like spooky fortune tellers. However, since we have just had a chapter on names and their importance to God, I want to take a quick look into what my name means to me.

I am calling this chapter "God's Presence" as a part of *little things* that can be *big things*. That is because too often we leave God out of the fact that parents can have an influence on their children if they prayerfully seek the Lord's presence and guidance in choosing a name for a child. I believe my parents did that for me. I was named after my great uncle Frank and my "adopted" uncle Watson.

Although I don't know a lot about my Grandmother Campbell's brother Frank, I know she admired him so much that she persuaded my mother and father to give their fourth child that name. If my memory serves me correctly, I believe I met my Uncle Frank in Newport News, Virginia, when I dropped my grandmother off there on my way to BJU when I was a junior.

My grandmother had been adopted when she was very young, so the family tree is not always accurate. Grandma had a half-brother after her mother remarried, but I believe Frank was her real brother. I remember being very impressed with this very dignified gentleman who had accomplished a great deal in his life, and who loved the Lord with all his heart. I was delighted to know that I had been named after this man.

Knowing that the name Frank means "a free man" is very much related to my trusting Christ as my Savior and becoming *really free* at an early age. When my grandmother Campbell showed me John 3:16 and so clearly explained its meaning, this little boy of five exclaimed: "Grandma, if you had told me when I was four, I would have understood." Even to this day, 82 years later, I can vividly recall the sense of the presence of the Lord as I knelt by the couch in my grandmother's living room and opened my heart to the Savior that morning. In 1998 I went to that same house where I had been saved. I stopped in the living room and told the couple living there about my trusting Christ in that very room.

Just as there are varied meanings to some words, the same thing is true of names. There are other related meanings to the name Frank that seem to show themselves now and then in my life. One definition says the name can mean "to have compassion for others." That even shows up in my spiritual gift of exhortation, consolation, or encouragement. The Greek word is *paraklesis* or *paraclete*, and it signifies one who comes along side of others to help make them successful. I am very much aware that just about everything I do is related to that motivation in me, whether I am teaching, conducting a choir, leading congregational singing, preaching, counseling, or doing any other type of ministry. Even my book, *Just Show Up: God Can Use You*, demonstrates that characteristic of my service for the Lord. I did not do much except encourage someone, and the Lord has used that for His glory.

My father's best friend during the 1920s in Bethel Bible School in Newark, New Jersey, was Watson Argue. He was already a gifted speaker at that time, and he and my Dad became close friends. "Uncle" Watson was also a trombone player and he always seemed to have money from his preaching engagements as a Bible student. He was also very generous, and he shared that money with my father. This, along with his friendship, made him very special to Dad who evidently never had any money, coming from a family of twelve. Watson's last name was "Argue," but I am happy my parents did not add that to my name since I definitely do not like to argue.

The name Watson was an early nickname for Walter that has a fascinating heritage. It had been the most common name in Scotland for many years. The first man with the name Watson came from England to the Virginia Colony in 1635. That date interests me because I know that my grandmother on my father's side of the family was Jessie Ward. Her ancestor, Andrew Ward, came to America in 1631, and he was known as "the founder of Connecticut." Henry *Ward* Beecher (a famous preacher during the civil war), Julia *Ward* Howe ("The Star-Spangled Banner"), William *Ward* Ayer (pastor of Calvary Baptist Church in New York City, 1936-1949), and Samuel *Ward* ("America the Beautiful"), all came from that family line.

A related meaning of Watson is "a desire to learn deeper truths." Even to this day I have a desire to learn more about many things, but especially the "deep truths" of the Word of God. I also love studying hymns and anything else that relates to music.

In addition, I enjoy learning other people's names and using them in conversations with them. It is amazing how much better waiters and waitresses (and others who serve) treat you when you learn and use their names. That has given me many opportunities for testimony to them as well. Names can be important, especially if you use the name of the person you are addressing, whether it is a waiter or waitress, a caregiver, or anyone else who does something for you.

Chapter 23

✦

HEARING AND DOING

Our Savior, the Lord Jesus Christ, is the wisest Teacher that has ever lived on this earth. I say "is" because he still *is* our wisest teacher if we will follow and obey His teaching. He could always see through a situation and address the core of the problem or the question that was being asked.

The first illustration of this is at the close of the Sermon on the Mount where the Lord sums up everything that He has taught in that quintessential sermon: the beatitudes, the similitudes or metaphors, the law, real religion, prayer, riches, trust, judging, righteousness, false teachers, faith, and foundations. As a teacher myself, I always tried at the conclusion of my sermon or lesson to sum up what I had taught, and I believe I learned this from studying Christ's methods.

Let's examine our Lord's summation of this greatest of sermons. He portrays his teaching with a masterful illustration of the difference between simply doing and both hearing and doing (His illustrations were always perfect). He begins with the same expansive word that he uses with Nicodemus in John 3:16: *whosoever*. That means you and I can each put our name in there, just as my grandmother had me do when I trusted Christ at five years of age: "whosoever" was anyone Grandma was leading to Christ, and that included me. She made it personal to help me understand.

The Lord at the end of Matthew 7 then gives an illustration that every person in the world has experienced at one time or another: a storm. In this case He related it to how a house has been built. As I mentioned earlier, our daughter Gina's husband David makes his living inspecting houses in Florida to determine whether they can withstand the hurricanes that devastate that state. If David endorses it, the owner gets a reduction in insurance costs.

Notice how the Lord so graphically describes the storm: the rains descended (*katabaino*, literally beyond measure or mightily, perhaps several inches an hour); the floods came (an overwhelming storm surge that destroys everything in its path); the winds blew (*anemos*, literally as if from the four quarters of the earth). Notice that the same kind of "hurricane" slams into both houses in this illustration.

Christ then closes His illustration with what most people would call a *little thing*, the part of the house that is never seen—the foundation. We will examine this further in the next chapter, but at this point let me mention what the Lord says is the difference between success and failure: both hearing and doing.

This brings us to what I believe is the crux of what has happened to Christians in many fundamental churches today. We are all good hearers of the Word. We say "Amen" to what the pastor admonishes us to do, but there is a disconnect between what we *hear* and what we *do*. The things of the world or our own concerns come between us and the truth we have heard, so that we fail to *do* what we should.

We may even *talk* about and affirm what we believe, but we seldom get around to *doing* and applying the truth to our everyday lives.

Christ used a very strong Greek word to describe what I have just mentioned. The Greek word for "foolish" is *moros*, from which our word "moron" comes. Strong's Concordance defines it as "dull or stupid, heedless, blockheaded, absurd." In other words, God says that when we fail to apply truth to our hearts and lives and we live without a consciousness of God's presence in every situation, we are spiritual morons.

Let's accept Christ's admonition and seek to be wise (thoughtful, sagacious, discreet, cautious) as verse 24 tells us we should be, so that God can bless us as He always wants to. In a couple of the next chapters we will relate stories about Christians who have done just that, and how God has blessed them.

Chapter 24

WISE AND FOOLISH

In the last chapter we mentioned how Strong's Concordance defines both foolish (*moros*, "dull or stupid, heedless, blockhead, absurd") and wise (*phronimos*, "thoughtful, sagacious, discreet, cautious") as in Matthew 7:24, 26. In this chapter I want to enlarge on that idea and apply it to how we serve the Lord in the *little things* of our lives.

The concept of being wise or having wisdom is used in the Bible over 650 times. In other words, wisdom is important to God. Therefore, when Jesus closed the Sermon on the Mount by giving a cogent illustration of how to be wise, He was instructing His disciples, all the numberless throng of people who were there, and all of *us* His followers, that we are not to be "morons" concerning spiritual things, but wise.

All of us have known people who appear to be foolish, and we ourselves have all acted foolishly as well at times. God knows that, and I believe He has made provision for our human frailty. It is no surprise to God when we fail because of the weakness of our flesh.

I believe I was able to express that in *My Life Is Thine*, the song I wrote while kneeling down by a bed in the motel before I was to speak to a group that I was told did not want to hear my message. (See pp. 100-101 in *I Being in the Way, the Lord Led Me* or Vignette 21 in *Just Show Up: God Can Use You*.)

Knowing that I was not sufficient for the situation that was confronting me, and realizing that I could accomplish nothing in my own strength, I knelt before the Lord and begged for His strength with these words:

> *Lord Jesus, I give Thee everything;*
> *Lord Jesus, but to Thy cross I cling.*

The last stanza of that song says,

> *Lord Jesus, although my flesh is weak,*
> *Lord Jesus, it is Thy will I seek.*

That fits right in here with what our Savior said about being wise: build our lives on Him, because He is our strength.

I don't remember what the response to my message was that night 40 years ago, but I know there were many of those rallies during the 1970s when, because there was a large group of unsaved young people there, between 50 and 70 came forward for salvation. That told me then, and still tells me now, that if the unsaved are there when the gospel is presented, God will use it to bring forth fruit for His glory. Those young people came to hear someone speak about music, and they ended up trusting Christ when the musician they came to hear gave them the truth of the gospel.

Another song that comes to my mind is one of my early "Patch the Pirate" songs. That song expresses the same idea with these words about God:

He's so great and I'm so small,
He's so strong and I'm so weak.

Wisdom comes when we realize that we cannot accomplish things in our own strength and need to rely on the power of God. Foolishness is thinking that we can rely on our own ability, our own persuasiveness, our own talent, or anything else of our own. God does not need any of these weak things of the flesh. He is just looking for someone to be faithful in trusting Him to use human, feeble efforts for His glory. That shows wisdom!

Chapter 25

A STRONG FOUNDATION

There are so many places in the world where a Bible principle is considered a *little thing* and is ignored, and the result is a catastrophe. This principle was important even in laying the foundation of the temple that Solomon built when God gave him special wisdom (1 Kings 4:29-34, 5:17-18, and 7:9-10). This was also emphasized in the restoration of the temple under Cyrus, the king of Persia (Ezra 3:10-12). The music that attended the revival that came at that same time must have been tremendous because the Scripture says it "was heard afar off."

Isaiah foretells more than 700 years before Christ that the Lord God will:

> *lay in Zion for a foundation a stone, a tried stone, a precious corner stone, a sure foundation: he that believeth shall not make haste* (Isaiah 28:16).

Isaiah is prophetically emphasizing that faith in Christ is the primary condition of salvation. Notice that this foundation is a *stone*, firm and able to support whatever is built over it. It is a *tried stone*, a chosen stone that is approved of God. It is also a *corner stone*, binding together the whole building and bearing the whole weight, a sure foundation on which to build. The wonderful effect of faith in Christ is that it is a foundation that also quiets and calms the soul.

In 1 Corinthians 3:10-11 the Apostle Paul emphasizes the necessity of a sure foundation, and that salvation is the only one that can be adequate. It is the Lord Jesus Christ Himself, not a *little thing* of man's imagination. Listen to the words of Paul:

> *According to the grace of God which is given unto me, as a wise masterbuilder I have laid the foundation, and another buildeth thereon. But let every man take heed how he buildeth thereupon. For other foundation can no man lay than that is laid, which is Jesus Christ.*

It is enlightening to read that Abraham, who was a wealthy man and could have lived in a beautiful home in his day, chose to live in a tent in the Promised Land. A tent is something movable; it does not take root anywhere. We learn here that possessions were not important to Abraham; he offered up his all to God. Abraham still possessed cattle and sheep and many other things, but because of his dedication of everything he owned to God, he had chosen to become a tent dweller. The foundation of his life was not in things, but in God.

I am also thinking today (March 25, 2018), about some close friends, Pastor David Yearick and his wife Bobbie, whom we knew and loved for over 65 years before they passed away recently. David took the Hampton Park Baptist Church from a very small church in 1964, and until 2000 when he retired, he shepherded it to what became a large ministry. However, they lived in a small house at

32 Kendal Green here in Greenville all 36 years. No matter how large the ministry became, they were satisfied to live in that same little house. Two other close friends, Bob and Nancy Shelton, have lived in a small house in Greenville for over 45 years, while their ministry has reached thousands for Christ.

The writer of the book of Hebrews makes this principle succinctly clear in Hebrews 11:8-10:

> *By faith Abraham, when he was called to go out into a place which he should after receive for an inheritance, obeyed; and he went out, not knowing whither he went. By faith he sojourned in the land of promise, as in a strange country, dwelling in tabernacles with Isaac and Jacob, the heirs with him of the same promise. For he looked for a city which hath foundations, whose builder and maker is God.*

We see here Abraham's gigantic faith, and that of other servants of the Lord, which enabled them to see beyond their present surroundings to a city in the future that God is preparing for those who love Him. Notice that it is a city with foundations that are built and made by God Himself. Just as the Apostle Paul in 1 Corinthians 3 called himself a wise master builder, God is the only one wise enough to build the city that is described in the book of Revelation.

Commentaries disagree on the dimensions of the holy Jerusalem that descends out of heaven from God, but suffice it to say here that it will be marvelous beyond any human comprehension. The description that John gives of it in Revelation 21 defies anyone to try to understand how great is the God of the known universe, with its billions of stars and unlimited space. We can rejoice in knowing that the foundations of that city (Revelation 21:14, 19) are laid by our wise Master Builder, the Lord Jesus Christ, who is the only one who can make things absolutely perfect.

All things were created by Him, and for Him (Colossians 1:16).

Chapter 26

A WISE BUILDER

As I mentioned earlier, David Greene is married to our daughter Gina. David has been a builder of many fine homes and is now an inspector in the panhandle of Florida. If David verifies that a home is built to withstand a hurricane, the owners will receive a significant deduction in their insurance costs. I recently asked David exactly how he does this, and here is what he basically told me about how he does his job.

The first thing that I noticed about what David explained to me was that there are seven things that he looks for when inspecting a house in what is called a "Uniform Mitigation Verification Inspection." I doubt that it was planned that way, but seven is the number of completion: our week has seven days, Sunday through Saturday; the next Sunday is number eight, the number of a new beginning; our musical scale has seven notes; using the white keys from C to B, the next C is number eight, a new beginning. When David completes his inspection, the homeowner is experiencing a kind of new beginning, reduced insurance rates in Florida.

In abbreviated form, here are the seven things David looks for:

1. **The Building Code** requires the age of the building: when the house was built and what building code it was in compliance with.

2. **The Roof Covering** must include all roof covering types in use, the product approval number or year of original installation or replacement.

3. **The Roof Deck Attachment** requires knowing what is the **weakest** form of roof attachment: the "mean uplift resistance" of the material being used.

4. **The Roof to Wall Attachment** requires a knowledge of the connection of the roof to walls. This includes the angle of the toe nails and how they are attached to the truss.

5. **The Roof Geometry** refers to the roof shape: whether it is a hip roof, a flat roof, or some other kind of roof.

6. **Secondary Water Resistance** refers to a supplemental means to protect the dwelling from water intrusion in the event of a roof covering loss. This is about what happens to the inside of the home if the basic roof is gone.

7. **Opening Protection Level** could be considered one of the most important considerations in the inspection process. There are many things to be considered, including both unverified shutter systems and wood structural panels meeting requirements for doors.

All of these *little things* may seem very complex to the average person, but to the inspector who does this many hours of every day, it becomes an almost automatic response to the quality of the construction of the building he is examining. He knows almost instinctively whether or not the building will withstand the forces of a hurricane. Everything in the building must be anchored to a *strong foundation*.

I cannot help thinking how this applies to the Christian life. Our foundation to which everything is anchored is the Word of God, and our trust in the Lord Jesus Christ. Our covering is the blood that was shed on the cross to protect us from the ravages of sin around us. The protecting walls are the fellowship we enjoy with other Christians and our accountability to those who trust us. The geometry of the covering is our testimony that does not give in to the pressures of the trials that come to all of us. The openings are the windows of our eyes and ears that must be protected from all the evils that surround us and try to lead us astray from following what we know to be true.

Let us make the Wise Master Builder the center of all we do, and let us allow Him to control every *little thing* of our Christian life and testimony for His glory.

Chapter 27

THE GIFT OF MEMORY

In today's society, we don't memorize enough. One way to increase memory is to write things down. Just the act of writing something down can help you to remember it. Another mnemonic device that I have come across and taught in memorizing Scripture is to write down the first letter of each word of a verse or a whole passage. You will be amazed how much that will help you to memorize and repeat it. Our family memorized whole books of the Bible that way as our children were growing up.

God wants us to remember things that He has done for us. He told the Israelites in Exodus 13:3 that He wanted them to remember all that he had done for them. God knew that we, like the Israelites, tend to forget the many good things He has done for us because we consider them to be *little things*.

> *Remember this day in which ye came out from Egypt, out of the house of bondage; for by strength of hand the LORD brought you out from this place.*

The foremost New Testament example of a good memory would be Stephen, a deacon in the early church, giving a detailed history of the Israelites as the Holy Spirit brought the Scriptures to his re-membrance. Forty-six percent of the verses in Stephen's sermon are quotations from the Old Testament (Acts 7:2-53). He remembered many *little things*.

Over the years I have met people who have tremendous memories. I am thinking of Dr. Monroe Parker who became a cherished friend. I first saw him in January of 1949 when I arrived at Bob Jones University. At that time, the faculty sat at tables of eight as the host and hostess for the six students who also sat there. I may have been introduced to Dr. Parker then, I don't know. However, I know that for some years at the university he held several key offices, including Dean of Students, Dean of Men, and Director of the Ministerial Class of over a thousand.

If you can ever find a copy of his book, *My First 77 Years*, you will be amazed at the memory that God gave that man. He remem-bered places, people, dates, call letters of radio stations on which he preached, the radio frequency of those stations, when he was there, and so on—many years after the events occurred.

In his messages, Dr. Parker would quote reams of passages of Scripture, long involved poems, detailed commentaries, Shakespeare, and historical facts from many periods of time. I asked him one time how he did it, thinking that I might learn something. His reply was that he didn't know; he just did it.

Let me give you one illustration that will demonstrate the memory of that man. Many years ago, he spoke at the Southside Baptist Church in Greenville, SC, where I was the minister of music. After he preached the message that morning, I told him what a blessing it was to me. Here was his reply: "I preached that message the first time I met you!" He not only knew where he had preached that message, but he knew I had been there one time when he did.

Some people have told me that they think I have an unusual memory. That may be true since I have conducted scores of pieces of music including ten operas completely from memory. However, I have to admit that it is hard work for me. I do it because I love it. As I have gotten older, my memory is like Swiss cheese: it has holes in it, sometimes very large ones. I like what my granddaughter Megan said to me when I told her that: "Yes, but it is aged to perfection!"

Some people have selective memories: they remember only what they want to remember. Others have periodic memory: it comes and goes in intervals. Still others have specialized memories. Kim Peek is a walking encyclopedia. He has memorized more than 7,600 books. He can recite the highways that go to each American city, town, or county, along with the area and zip codes, the television stations, and the telephone networks that serve them. But he is a savant who is not able to function normally.

Most of us can thank the Lord that he gave us the ability to remember the things that really matter while not being concerned that we cannot remember some of the things we wish we could. Memory is definitely a gift from the Lord to be cherished and used wisely.

Go back to the beginning of this chapter and begin to use some of the suggestions I mentioned there: write things down, write what God has done for you, and use the mnemonic device of using the first letters of each word in a Scriptural verse or passage to remember it. There are so many varied things going *through* our minds these days that we need to focus on the things that God considers important.

In addition to the ideas in the last paragraph, invest your life in other people, and you will be surprised at what God will teach you as you live your life for others.

Chapter 28

🐦

THE GIFT OF FORGETTING

This may seem like a strange topic, especially since it can be embarrassing and very inconvenient to forget something you really want to remember: someone's name; an important meeting; a wedding of a close friend; or where you put something you desperately need. These are not all *little things*.

However, like almost every other bad thing, there can be a good side to being able to forget something. I think the most salient example I can give of this is what Isaiah quotes God as saying:

> *I, even I, am he that blotteth out thy transgressions for mine own sake, and **will not remember thy sins*** (Isaiah 43:25).

> *I have blotted out, as a thick cloud, thy transgressions, and, as a cloud, thy sins: return unto me, for I have redeemed thee* (Isaiah 44:22).

We should rejoice that God promises to forget our transgressions and sins. That also means that if we are to be "conformed to the image of [Christ]" (Romans 8:29), we should be forgetting the sins that have been committed against us as well.

Instead of constantly bringing up the failures and the sins of the past, we should do what the Apostle Paul said he would do in Philippians 3:13-14:

> *This one thing I do, forgetting those things which are behind, and reaching forth unto those things that are before, I press toward the mark for the prize of the high calling of God in Christ Jesus.*

Have you ever thought of all the things that Paul had to forget? As he said in 1 Corinthians 15:9-10:

> *I am the least of the apostles, that am not meet to be called an apostle, because I persecuted the church of God. But by the grace of God I am what I am: and his grace which was bestowed upon me was not in vain: but I labored more abundantly than they all: yet not I, but the grace of God which was with me.*

Or consider Paul's testimony before a heathen king, Agrippa, in which he outlines all the wrong things he did before he was saved. He evidently did not consider them to be *little things*.

> *I verily thought with myself, that I ought to do many things contrary to the name of Jesus of Nazareth. Which thing I also did in Jerusalem: and many of the saints did I shut up in prison, having received authority from the chief priests; and when they were put to death, I gave my voice against them. And I punished them oft in every synagogue, and compelled them to blaspheme; and being exceedingly mad against them, I persecuted them even unto strange cities* (Acts 26:9-11).

Here Paul is telling this unbelieving king all the things he had to forget in order to try to make the king see that any sinner could be saved if he would trust in the Savior that Paul had trusted. We could be more effective in our testimonies if we would follow Paul's example.

Another testimony like this was what Joseph did when his first son was born in Egypt. He called the boy Manasseh (*forgetting*), and then he explains why:

> *For God hath made me forget all my toil, and all my father's house* (Genesis 41:51).

On the surface, we may think Joseph didn't care. But what he is saying is that he is deliberately "forgetting" all the wrongs that had been done to him back home by his brothers, and then their selling him as a slave. He then forgot the wrongs that Potiphar and his wife had done in unjustly putting him in prison. He also never tried to get even with anyone including the chief butler who forgot him for *two long years*. Retaliation was not a part of Joseph's character.

We should perhaps also try to be careful in confessing things that other people have forgotten. I had a woman do that recently. She apologized for something that she had said that she thought hurt me, but I cannot for the life of me remember what it was about.

May God help us to copy Paul's and Joseph's responses and consciously forget all the injustices, omissions, oversights, and deliberate wrongs that have come our way, and let God do all that He wants to do through us.

Chapter 29

THE IMPORTANCE OF REST

If our omnipotent Almighty God rested "on the seventh day from all his work that he had made," rest must be an *important thing* for all human beings who are made in his image (Genesis 2:2). The very next verse goes on to expand on the importance of rest:

And God blessed the seventh day, and sanctified it: because that in it he had rested from all his work which God created and made (Genesis 2:3).

Scripture uses a comparison of how the Israelites failed for forty years to enter into the rest that God had for them in the Promised Land, and the failure was because of their unbelief. The extended passage in Hebrews 3:18-4:11 explains what God wants His children to do to enjoy the rest He has promised them.

Let's look at the phrases that God uses to speak of the rest He wants us to have and how Christians can "come short of" it:

the word preached did not profit them, not being mixed with faith (4:2);

as I have sworn in my wrath, if they shall enter into my rest (4:3);

and God did rest the seventh day from all his works (4:4);

if they shall enter into my rest (4:5);

they to whom it was first preached entered not in because of unbelief (4:6);

today, if ye will hear his voice, harden not your hearts (4:7);

if Jesus had given them rest, then he would not have spoken of another day (4:8);

there remaineth therefore a rest to the people of God (4:9);

he also hath ceased from his own works, as God did from his (4:10);

let us labor therefore to enter into that rest, lest any man fall after the same example of unbelief (4:11).

In the previous verses where the word *rest* is used ten times and in other places in the Bible, God wants us to know the rest He has promised us. For instance, the book of Ruth is a classic illustration of the rest that God wants His people to have. It must be remembered where the story of Ruth comes in the Bible narrative. This jewel comes right after the book of Judges, which ends with this statement: "every man did that which was right in his own eyes." In addition to that, Ruth was a Moabite, married into a backslidden family, with no seeming chance of ever finding rest.

In the first two chapters of the book about her, we find Ruth deciding to follow God faithfully with what little knowledge of Him she must have had. We then find her serving her mother-in-law with a devotion that very few young women ever exhibit. However, we have to wait until Chapter 3 of Ruth to see how she obtains the rest that God had intended for her.

Naomi tells Ruth that she intends to "seek rest" for her that "it may be well with thee." The instructions that Naomi gives to Ruth would not only have startled any young woman, it would have scared most daughters-in-law out of their wits. This would be true, especially if they, like Ruth, did not know the Jewish customs that existed at that time. Ruth had to completely obey everything her mother-in-law asked her to do without asking any questions.

She had to wash herself, anoint herself with oil, put special clothes on, go down to the threshing floor, not make herself known, mark the place where Boaz would be, and lie down at Boaz's feet (Ruth 3:1-4). Amazing! This required *pure, comprehensive submission* for Ruth.

In verse seven of that chapter we learn the key to finding rest: *complete obedience*! Notice what Ruth says,

> *All that thou sayest unto me I will do* (Ruth 3:7).

Most people want the rest without the obedience, but it never works that way. Obedience always precedes reward! Also notice that the sixth verse of that chapter says,

> *She went down unto the floor, and did according to all that her mother in law bade her.*

The remainder of the book of Ruth shows the remarkable rest that God gave her. That night Boaz spoke kindly to her and called her his daughter; he promised to do "all that she requires"; he also promised "to do the part of a kinsman"; and he gave her a large portion of barley to give to her mother-in-law. Matthew Henry quotes Bishop

Hall as saying: "Boaz blessed her as a father, encouraged her as a friend, promised her as a kinsman, rewarded her as a patron, sent her away laden with hopes and gifts, no less chaste, more happy than she came" (p. 279, verb forms adjusted).

The unexcelled "rest" that Ruth received was to marry Boaz, have a son, and become the great-grandmother of David. About 1300 years later, she is listed in the book of Matthew along with Rahab, her other mother-in-law (Boaz's mother), as being in the line of Christ Himself. There is no way that Ruth could ever have imagined that over 3,000 years later, we would be studying her dedication to do God's will, His blessing on her life, and the overflowing, eternal *rest* that only He could give her.

Chapter 30

Rests in Music

Music is such a good illustration of life that much can be learned about life by studying music theory. The term "music theory" can be a little misleading because it is not only "theory," but a study of what constitutes good music. One of the flaws of rock music is that there are no places for rests in the way it is put together. It is a constant, overwhelming cacophony of loud sound.

The average person who has never studied how great composers wrote their music is not likely to understand how important rests are. The idea of having rests may seem like an unimportant *little thing* in music. However, they are a major characteristic of music that is well written.

Here are just a few examples of why rests are important to music: to break the monotony of the sound; to change the tempo of the music; to change the pitch or the key of the music; to change direction; to make a deliberate pause; and to keep the other notes from stringing together in a breathless and chaotic way. All these things are a vital part of musical structure. Even the Psalms in the "hymnbook" of the Old Testament use pauses (*Selah*) or rests in them that make them more meaningful.

All singers and any musicians who play an instrument that requires breath know how important the rests are. There must be rests so that the performer can catch his breath. If the music continues incessantly, the performer will wear out quickly. One of the first things any of these musicians must learn is how to breathe correctly. Many years of concentrated study are dedicated to learning to properly work the breathing apparatus that the Lord has placed in our bodies. Without this knowledge, the tone of the voice or of the instrument will never be what it should be.

This is not only true of woodwind and brass instruments; it is also true of string and keyboard instruments. If you watch the string section of any preeminent orchestra, you will notice how all the string players breathe together so that the natural rest places in the music, whether they are marked or not, happen simultaneously. Watching and listening to concert pianists and organists reveal that they are feeling the music so intensely that they place rests where they belong so that the message of the music comes through. No piece of music would be complete without a balance of notes and rests. Both are important.

This is also true of time. We take it for granted, but think how our hours, days, and weeks would all be blurred together if time were not divided the way God has designed it. We have light and darkness to separate day and night; we have weekends that are supposed to give us a break from work; Sundays are intended to be a day of rest, and a part of people's frustration today is because they have neglected that rhythm. We even have seasons that divide our years. People who live in the polar regions of the earth have difficulty because in their summers the days are too long, and in the winters the nights seem to go on forever.

A good comparison with which we are familiar should show why rests are important in music. Music is like a language because it communicates. Imagine yourself listening to a speaker who never takes a breath between sentences or even phrases. Just the idea shows how ludicrous this would be.

Even in written language, we have periods, commas, question marks, exclamation points, and several other forms of punctuation that demonstrate the fact that there are pauses or rests in our thinking processes as we read out loud or even silently. Poems are divided into stanzas, and prose is divided into paragraphs.

A further comparison would be playing periods in sports. The playing period is a division of time in sports or games in which play occurs. Many games are divided into a fixed number of periods, which may be named for the number of divisions (e.g., a half or a quarter). Other games use terminology independent of the total number of divisions (e.g., sets or innings). A playing period may have a fixed length of game time or be bound by other rules (e.g., three outs in baseball or a sudden-death goal in overtime). Baseball is also divided into at bats and innings; football is divided into downs and quarters; and basketball and soccer each have two halves. These are all divided to give the players time to rest between the periods of activity.

Our books of the Bible are divided into chapters and verses to make them easier to memorize and to help us find the thoughts and principles that God wants us to know. Building on these divisions, many Bibles have concordances to help us find the verses we are trying to remember. Without these "rests," our knowledge would all run together and be unavailable to us. We should be grateful for all rests, especially musical rests.

Vignette 22 of *Just Show Up: God Can Use You* has an interesting discussion of rests in music by Juan Marcos Martinez on page 123.

Chapter 31

A Slingshot

We live at a time when weapons are debated. Some people think that because crime is so rampant, no one should have guns. Others think that if lawful citizens can have guns, they can defend themselves against those who would desire to do them harm.

The purpose of this chapter is to show that the Bible teaches that it is not the weapon that is important. It is the mindset and intentions of the person with the weapon that make the difference. In the spiritual realm, it is not the size of the weapon but the purpose of the weapon holder and his trust in God that determine the outcome of any spiritual battle.

You probably have determined where I am going with this and are wondering why I would use such a familiar story between two people to illustrate a point. The reason is that this battle between just two people is the most famous battle in all of the Old Testament. It also shows how important *little things* can be in any situation.

The most important *little thing* is what a film about Esther has her say concerning David and Goliath: "David won the battle, not because he fought well, but *because he believed well*."

Let's look at the differences between the two combatants. The first thing we notice is that their preparation was different. Goliath was "a man of war from his youth," and David was just a teenager (1 Samuel 17:33, 42). Next, Goliath had lots of armor: a coat of mail (a jacket covered with or composed of metal rings or plates, serving as armor), 175 to 200 pounds; a brass helmet and leggings; a brass spear with a head of 20-25 pounds; superior height, being nine to ten feet tall; and a servant to carry his shield (17:4-7). David had only a shepherd's coat, a slingshot, and some stones that he picked up from the brook (17:40).

Next, Goliath had much experience. He had won many victories over the enemies of the Philistines. He was their champion. David's experience was out on the hillsides as a young shepherd. He had protected his sheep from a lion and a bear that he had "caught by his beard, and smote him, and slew him" (17:34-36). He had evidently done that with his bare hands, not even with a weapon.

But that brings us to the most important points of the story. Goliath was a confident braggart who cursed David "by his gods." He thought he was invincible to any challenger. David was a humble innocent boy whose trust was in "the LORD of hosts, the God of the armies of Israel." He was not a soldier. He had never even fought a military battle. Man looks on the outward appearance, but God looks on the heart.

Goliath was so proud and arrogant that he thought he could not be beaten. However, in spite of his helmet, at least a little of his forehead showed. That was where David's accuracy and God's guidance put the stone. Only one stone, a *little thing*, was needed to penetrate into the very little place that was unprotected. Perhaps David had selected five stones in case Goliath had four brothers. I like the way God sometimes emphasizes things (and even "rubs it in") when verse 50 says, "So David prevailed over the Philistine *with a sling and with a stone,* and smote the Philistine, and slew him; *but there was no sword in the hand of David.*"

It is interesting to notice that the description of Goliath and his armament (17:4-7) does not mention the sword that David had to use to cut off Goliath's head after he fell on his face. That sword must have been heavy as well, but David had no trouble using it when it was needed. Ron Hamilton's song about this battle is exactly right when it says that "God is bigger than giants are, and He can kill them all!" All that David needed were three *little things* that God used to give him and the Israelites the victory that day: his trust in the Lord, a small stone, and a slingshot!

Chapter 32

BATTLES

I must say at the beginning of this chapter that I do not like battles. I was not born to be a soldier like one of my best friends for over 60 years, Major Ron Brooks. Until Ron went to be with His Lord on January 11, 2017 at almost 80 years of age, Ron approached all of life as a good soldier.

However, I cannot dodge the fact that the Bible commands every one of us who know Him to face the battles that come to all of us as Christians. The Apostle Paul warned the Ephesians that they needed to be strong in the Lord and put on *the whole armor of God* because there is a battle to be fought (Ephesians 6:10-18). He also admonished Timothy, his son in the faith, that he needed to "fight the good fight of faith" (1 Timothy 6:12).

When I began exposing worldly, sensual music in 1965, I knew that I was going to more than likely face some opposition. When that same music began coming into Christian schools and colleges, I began to realize that the opposition was going to come from places I never had expected.

At that time in my ministry, I began to make a study of men of the past who have had to face the same kind of challenges, some of which were much fiercer than mine. This made me realize mine were nothing (*little things*) in comparison. One of my favorite books at that time was *Foxe's Book of Martyrs*. This book was first published in English in 1563 by John Day. It includes a vivid account of the sufferings of Protestants under the Catholic Church, with particular emphasis on England and Scotland. Here is just one quotation from that book:

> *"On the death of Leo X in 1521, Adrian, the inquisitor general, was elected pope. He had laid the foundation of his papal celebrity in Spain. It appears, according to the most moderate calculation, that during the five years of the ministry of Adrian, 24,025 persons were condemned by the inquisition, of whom* **one thousand six hundred and twenty were burned alive.***"*

I hesitate to even mention one of my own experiences since it pales in the light of the facts above. However, I am confident that some of my readers of this book will relate my experience to some of theirs that seemed to be overwhelming when they occurred. Looking back, I just want to thank my Lord for His manifest presence with me in what could have been a battle or at least an overwhelming circumstance.

I was attending a Christian educators' conference in Tampa, Florida. Dr. Bob Moore, a pastor in Marietta, Georgia, came to me and told me his situation. He had invited a Charismatic speaker to come to his church for a special meeting, but when the speaker arrived, he brought a Christian rock band with him. When Pastor Moore told the speaker he could not have the rock band perform in the service, the speaker said, "If you can't have my rock band, you can't have me," and he left.

Pastor Moore said he had 2,000 people coming to the meeting that night and he wanted me to go and speak to them about why he could not have the rock band. I replied, "You are throwing me to the wolves!" When Pastor Moore insisted, I thought I had a way out by saying, "If you can get me a plane ticket up there tonight and another back down here tomorrow morning, I will go." He got the tickets!

As I was sitting on the platform that evening in front of 2,000 eager people, the man at the podium announced that I was speaking instead of the Charismatic man. About 1,000 people got up and walked out on the spot. As I began to speak, there was a constant exit of people leaving for the next 30 minutes or so. I never got upset nor said anything about what was happening. (God had to be helping me!)

Somewhere during that time, God took over my mind and said, "Don't talk about music as Pastor Moore asked you to; just give the people who are still here the gospel." As I obeyed God's prompting, the Holy Spirit had to fill my mouth, because I launched into the powerful message of the Gospel. I wish I could remember all I said, because when I gave the invitation at the end, 50 to 60 people came forward to trust the Lord as their Savior. Now, they may have been Charismatic people getting saved the second time, but that was God's business, not mine. There was no way I could have prepared for that occasion.

I have had many events like these over the years, but a similar one is on page 101 of *I Being in the Way, the Lord Led Me*, and another two are in Chapter 14 of this book.

Chapter 33

YOUR PRIVATE LIFE

Too often, we consider our private life not to be as important as our public image. That concept is based on the false premise that what people think about us is more important what we know ourselves to be. In other words, we consider our private life to be a *little thing*. We don't take enough time to study the word of God, to pray, and to meditate on Scriptural principles. By doing this, we deceive ourselves into thinking we do not have enough time for these things because of the pressing issues of the day.

This chapter is based on a sermon that I heard given by Jim Schettler, a good friend of mine, when he and I were the preachers at the Berean Baptist Church Bible Conference, Lilburn, Georgia, in 1999. It is a concept that I learned from Pastor Schettler that is like many other things I learned from this gifted preacher and real man of God.

The title of his message that day in June was, *Our Private Life Should Be Equal to Our Public Image*. I will discuss the first part of that concept in this chapter and the second part in the next chapter. The outline is Jim's, but the expounding text is mine. The reason for including the principle in this book is because of how *little* the distance between the two things should be!

The first point is taken from Daniel 6:3.

> *This Daniel was preferred above the presidents and princes, because an excellent spirit was in him; and the king thought to set him over the whole realm.*

We must always be careful and cautious whenever we are being preferred or promoted to a higher position in life. As with both Joseph and Daniel, there are always going to be those around us who do not want us to be promoted. This quite often is also the time that the devil can use to make us think we are better than we actually are.

If you check the time line of Daniel's life, you will find that he is probably in his eighties when this test came to him. In other words, we never get to the point in our Christian life where we "have it made" and don't need to face the trials that come our way. Daniel is one of the few Bible characters who are consistent throughout their lives.

The reason that Daniel did not become proud was that in his private life there was *an excellent spirit inside him.* His private life made him fit for the public ministry and service that was coming his way. As Hudson Taylor said so succinctly, "God never works *through* a man until he works *in* a man."

The second point is from Daniel 6:4.

> *Then the presidents and princes sought to find occasion against Daniel concerning the kingdom; but they could find none*

occasion nor fault; forasmuch as he was faithful, neither was there any error or fault found in him.

Our private life is always in the view of heaven. Man can see only the outward appearance, but God knows the heart.

We see the same thing in Job 1:1, 8.

> *1. There was a man in the land of Uz, whose name was Job; and that man was perfect and upright, and one that feared God, and eschewed evil.*
>
> *8. And the LORD said unto Satan, Hast thou considered my servant Job, that there is none like him in the earth, a perfect and an upright man, one that feareth God, and escheweth evil?*

Verse one is basically his reputation with man, and verse eight is his reputation with God. What he was in his public image is exactly what he was in his private life.

The next point is from Daniel 6:5.

> *Then said these men, We shall not find any occasion against this Daniel, except we find it against him concerning the law of his God.*

Our private life is where the real battle rages. Martin Luther said, "The real battle rages in the very area that both Christ and Satan want." It could easily be the area in which we are successful, or the area where God has gifted us with ability. Any sin that we allow affects *every area* of our lives.

The next point is from Daniel 6:10-11.

> *Now when Daniel knew that the writing* [the decree of the king] *was signed, he went into his house; and his windows being open in his chamber toward Jerusalem, he kneeled upon his knees three times a day, and prayed, and gave thanks before his God, as he did aforetime. Then these men assembled, and found Daniel praying and making supplication before his God.*

Remember again, that Daniel at this point is probably at least eighty years old. He has served the Lord for a long time. He did not consider his private life *a little thing*. Our private life is what we really are! We can fool others and sometimes even ourselves, but that does not change anything. Sooner or later our private life does become public.

Chapter 34

YOUR PUBLIC IMAGE

We all need to be cautious in making sure that our public image is what we know ourselves to really be. Someone has said that flattery is a form of hatred. Quite often, the flatterer is expecting and hoping for a favor from the flattered person. When someone flatters us with lavish praise, they are not being kind to us. They are trying to create a public image that has nothing to do with reality.

The statements above are not intended to mean that we should not accept sincere compliments. When others are grateful for what we have done for them, when we have helped them in some way, or when we have gone out of our way to be kind to them, it is a natural thing for them to express gratitude and thankfulness. That is not what we are discussing here.

As a public speaker, I have periodically been introduced with lavish praise for what the Lord has allowed me to do. I have several quips that I like to use on those occasions. They are meant to be funny, but I believe they also get across a point that corrects what my public image should be. I might say, "May the Lord forgive us both: the person who introduced me for exaggerating so much, and me for enjoying it so much!" Or I might say, "The person who was just introduced couldn't be here, so I came in his place!"

I am reminded of a story about a chauffeur who worked for and traveled with a famous scientist. The scientist, in his lectures, used involved formulas and intricate systematic details of science that only a graduate of Massachusetts Institute of Technology could understand. One day as they were driving to a large university for a lecture, the chauffer said this to the scientist: "I have heard your lecture so often that I could give it as well as you do." To which the professor replied: "OK, wise guy. We are about the same size. Let's exchange clothes tonight and we will see how well you do."

The lecture went fine, but as soon as it was over, the moderator asked if there were any questions. One young intellectual college student asked the chauffer a very involved question about the lecture. The chauffer's reply was classic: "I am surprised that a college student would ask such a simple question. And just to show how simple the question was, I am going to let my chauffeur answer it!"

The point of the story is that it is very easy for us to think better of ourselves than we should. Romans 12:1-2 reminds us to give ourselves as a living sacrifice to God so that we can "prove what is that good, and acceptable, and perfect will of God." But the very next verse says, "To every man that is among you, *not to think of himself more highly than he ought to think* (Romans 12:3). Pride is not a *little thing*!

As I mentioned earlier, I recently had a friend say something to me that encouraged me greatly as a songwriter: "When I read or hear your songs, I see your heart." I was grateful because I really would like for people to know me as I am on the inside, not some public image they or others may have created.

May the Lord give each of us the wisdom to make our private life equal to our public image. This is a case where the unusual *little thing* is that the distance between the two should be difficult to find.

Chapter 35

WOLVES IN SHEEP'S CLOTHING

A good preacher or Bible expositor can take a complex concept and explain it such that everyone can understand it. A poor preacher or Bible expositor can take a simple concept and make it sound so complex that no one can grasp its meaning. The difference should be a *little thing*, but it is often very large.

Emet is the Hebrew word for truth, and (according to the website HavdalahDrasha.org) even the way the word is spelled in Hebrew sheds light on what truth actually is. *Aleph* is the first letter and it represents "the breath of God" or our awareness of Him. The middle letter *mem* was originally the symbol for water in Hebrew and it is also understood to represent the Messiah, *the fountain of life*. The final letter of *emet* is *tav*, which is the final letter of the alphabet. It is the expression of simple faith to the Hebrew.

Even the construction of the Hebrew word *truth* (made up of the first, middle, and last letters of the Hebrew alphabet) represents the stability in a life that is submitted to God and His wisdom. Since all things are made by Him and for Him (Colossians 1:16-17), it is not what man thinks but what the Bible so clearly teaches about salvation through the Lord Jesus Christ that is *truth*.

I remember hearing a so-called Bible scholar speak one time on some passage of the Bible that should have been made clear by his teaching it. However, he made his message so esoteric and abstruse that no one could even begin to understand what he was trying to get across. When he was finished, the man who had invited him to speak and was listening to his message said, "I don't know what this man just said, but I *agree with it*!" I remember thinking, That's no compliment!

I also remember an article that was in a magazine a number of years ago. The article was called "Beware the Illusion of Learning." It told of 55 psychiatrists, psychologists, and social workers who were to hear and judge a "doctor" speaking on a medical subject. The speaker was actually an actor who had no idea of what he was talking about. However, all these educated people who attended were fooled because the speaker knew how to communicate nonsense.

The Bible has a way of making things clear with just a few words. For instance: "In the beginning God created" (Genesis 1:1); "Be strong and of a good courage" (Joshua 1:9); "Every man did that which was right in his own eyes" (Judges 21:25); "Thy people shall be my people, and thy God my God" (Ruth 1:16); "Wisdom is the principal thing" (Prov. 4:7); "The Word was God" (John 1:1); "I am the way, the truth, and the life" (John 14:6); "Ye must be born again" (John 3:7); to mention just a few.

As I mentioned earlier, when my grandmother led me to the Lord when I was just five years old, she made it so clear that I told her that I would have understood it when I was four. God made His plan of salvation so simple that anyone can understand it. It is amazing how complex and unclear some people make it.

The Bible makes it plain that there are "some that trouble you, and would *pervert* the gospel of Christ" (Galatians 1:7). The next verse goes on to say that there are preachers that do that also. Jesus made it evident that there are "false prophets, which come to you in sheep's clothing, but inwardly they are ravening wolves" (Matthew 7:15).

What was happening in Jesus' time has been happening ever since. It may take different forms and approaches, but a classic example of this problem in our time is called neo-orthodoxy. These are preachers, churches, and movements that say they are preaching the gospel, but they are "wolves in sheep's clothing." They even use Bible passages and Bible words, but they change the *meaning* of the passages and words. Quite often, it is not so much what they say but what they leave out.

Martin Luther addressed this problem very succinctly 500 years ago:

> *If I protest with the loudest and the clearest exposition every portion of the truth of God, except precisely that little point which the world and the devil are at that moment attacking, I am not confessing Christ, however boldly I may be professing Christ.*

This is precisely what the wolves who pretend to be sheep do. They give just enough of the truth for undiscerning Christians to be fooled. It appears that many people who 50 years ago attended Bible-believing churches are now attending compromising churches whose pastoral leaders are in many cases wolves in sheep's clothing.

One of the most obvious examples of this trend is in the area of Christian music. If you are not familiar with that to which I am referring, may I suggest that you get a book that I have authored: *The Rock Generation: Six Decades of Decline*. In that book, I delineate how the fruit has fallen off the tree, but also how close to its source the fruit has fallen. The distance is *not* at all a *little thing*.

Things that seemed impossible six decades ago have come upon us like a tsunami. Many people, Christians included, are willingly ignorant of how the church has been overflowed with the water of compromise that has come in so rapidly (2 Peter 3:5-6). It seems logical to apply this Scripture to wolves in sheep's clothing since verse 3 says, "There shall come in the last days scoffers, walking after their own lusts" (2 Peter 3:3). The Greek word *scoffer* in that verse is *empaiktes*, which literally means "a false teacher." No other word could better describe a wolf in sheep's clothing.

Chapter 36

So Close!

This may seem like a strange chapter for *little things*, but having worked with and taught music for so many years makes me cognizant of how music can express reality in so many ways. If you have read *Just Show Up: God Can Use You*, you might remember Vignette #7 that shows how I applied Biblical principles to music theory as I was teaching at BJU. In this chapter we will see another musical principle that applies to reality.

It is difficult to explain the principle on paper, but I will try. I think any musician or someone who just loves music will understand what is involved. During the years that I spoke on music, it was easy to demonstrate "so close!" I would play a note on a piano and supposedly attempt to sing that note. However, instead of singing the note accurately and on pitch, I would sing just a little lower than the actual pitch.

For instance, if the note were A440, that means that the frequency of the note is 440 Hz. Or putting it differently, four hundred and forty sound waves are produced per second. If that is too technical for you, just remember that your eardrum picks up that frequency and your God-given brain sorts out the pitch and lets you know what the note is supposed to sound like. All players of string instruments know that A440 is the note to which they tune their instruments.

Now, when I am demonstrating this to an audience, I usually start by singing about 430Hz. All musicians in the audience cringe. The difference is obvious. However, when I gradually move my singing pitch up to 438Hz while still playing the correct note on the piano, the musicians go wild. They can't stand it! And the closer I get to the correct pitch, but still miss it, *the worse it is*. Not better—*worse*!

The point is: the closer you get to the *truth*, and still miss it, the worse it is. Not better—*worse*! And this is exactly what has happened in many circles. There are leaders in what is called Christendom today who are teaching terrible error, but they are coming "so close." People who do not really know their Bibles or who are only lukewarm Christians are deceived because they do not recognize the error.

Let's look at a couple of examples. In the preceding chapter, I mentioned neo-orthodoxy. Neo-orthodox ministers say they believe the Bible is the Word of God, but many of them believe Shakespeare's works are too. Ask a neo-orthodox person if Jesus is the Son of God and he will say "Yes." But if he is a hard-core believer of neo-orthodoxy, he could also believe that Jesus was the son of a German soldier with a Jewish girl.

He will probably tell you that as long as you have "faith," it doesn't make any difference. If you think I am exaggerating, the examples above came from some personal conversations I had with a neo-orthodox preacher many years ago.

Let me cite an example of what might seem to be "so close!" from a book about Islam that every Christian today should have. The book is called *Islam: Past, Present, Future: What Every Loyal American Needs to Know*, by Dr. Gene Gurganus.

> *Isa, the Koranic name for Jesus, is exalted in the Koran. He is said to be virgin born, sinless, the Word of God, the Messiah, a miracle worker.*

You say, What? That is in the Koran? Yes, it is! But look at what follows.

> *But he is only a man, only a prophet, and he did not die on the cross. Someone died on the cross but according to the Koran, it was not Jesus. Allah took Jesus to heaven and since Jesus has been in heaven, he has been converted into a Muslim* (Islam, p. 33).

If all you knew were the first quote, you would think that Islam is not that bad. However, the devil's counterfeit religion is keeping billions of people from knowing the Jesus of the Bible, who can save them from their sin. On the surface, it appears to come close, but the closer it comes, the worse it is!

I like the sub-title of the book by Dr. Gurganus, but I would like to alter it here at the close of this chapter: *What Every Born-again Christian Needs to Know*. The devil is a master counterfeiter and he knows how to come close to the truth.

When banks are training their tellers to recognize counterfeit money, they don't show them the counterfeits. They have them count real money over and over until they know what it feels like, so that the fake becomes obvious to them. We Christians need to know the Truth of the Word of God so thoroughly that any falsehood, no matter how close, will be obvious.

Chapter 37

✦

KEEPING THINGS IN BALANCE

Isn't it wonderful that our Almighty God loves us and uses us in spite of our weaknesses? We try to act as if God doesn't know how weak we are, and we think He is surprised when we do not do everything just right. Nothing could be farther from the truth. He is a great and wonderful God, and we can put our lives fully into His care.

One of the things that let us know that the Bible is the Word of God is that when His people fail and make mistakes, He does not gloss over their weaknesses. He includes the mistakes of some people in His Word so that we will know that we too can be used by Him in spite of how weak we are if we will submit to Him. We can then give Him the glory for anything that He has allowed us to accomplish.

When Majesty Music produced Majesty Hymns, we mentioned in its Preface that we were seeking "balance" in our selection of congregational songs to make the singing of churches alive, varied, and inspirational. We received correspondence that criticized us because the Bible does not mention the word "balance." However, as we wrote in the Preface, we believe the principle is taught in Scripture.

For instance, in reading and studying the four Gospels, we see that there is always friction between the Pharisees and the Sadducees. Jesus went right down the middle and criticized them both. Our Lord was balanced. To think, like the Pharisees, that keeping certain man-made rules makes us spiritual is inherently wrong. To deny the resurrection, as the Sadducees did, is also wrong.

It is illuminating to understand that much error is an over-emphasis on a truth. It is unbalanced. For instance, the Bible teaches much about our thinking process.

> *As [a man] thinketh in his heart, so is he* (Proverbs 23:7).

Or take this all-inclusive Scripture:

> *Finally, brethren, whatsoever things are true,*
> *whatsoever things are honest,*
> *whatsoever things are just,*
> *whatsoever things are pure,*
> *whatsoever things are lovely,*
> *whatsoever things are of good report,*
> *if there be any virtue,*
> *and if there be any praise,*
> ***think on these things*** (Philippians 4:8).

Are any of the things mentioned in this one verse *little things?"* I submit that each one, when taken by itself, is vitally important for any Christian who desires to grow into the image of Christ. As the Apostle Paul says,

*For whom he did foreknow, he also did predestinate to **be conformed to the image of his son**, that he might be the firstborn
among many brethren* (Romans 8:29).

*I count all things but loss for the excellency of the knowledge of
Christ Jesus my Lord: for whom I have suffered all things, and
do count them but dung, that I may win Christ, and be found
in him, not having mine own righteousness, which is of the law,
but that which is through the faith of Christ, the righteousness
which is of God by faith: that I may know him, and the power of
his resurrection, and the fellowship of his sufferings, being made
conformable unto his death; if by any means I might attain unto
the resurrection of the dead* (Philippians 3:8-11).

Notice that these verses are not talking about obtaining salvation.
They are teaching us that we as Christians must grow in grace as we
seek to become like Christ. However, there have been false teachers in the past and now in the present who would substitute what
Norman Vincent Peale called the "power of positive thinking."

As the pastor of the Marble Collegiate Church in New York City
for 52 years, Peale was the man who prepared the way for the large
churches of our day. He took existing ideas from Christian Science
and other false teachings, gave them a Biblical veneer, integrated
them with psychology, and packaged them for the masses, spreading
his message through his book *The Power of Positive Thinking*. He
taught phrases like:

"Believe in yourself!"
"Have faith *in your abilities!*"

"Have reasonable confidence *in your own powers.*"

I like what one commentator said about this false prophet:

"Peale is appalling, and Paul is appealing."

There is nothing of real salvation in any of this man's teaching. This kind of heresy has been prevalent for centuries, and it is still prevalent today. The Marble Collegiate Church grew to over 5,000 members, just as many popular churches have grown today. The people have "itching ears" and "will not endure sound doctrine" (2 Timothy 4:3). May God deliver us from this kind of preacher!

Chapter 38

DON'T MAKE BIG THINGS OUT OF INSIGNIFICANT THINGS

You may wonder why this title is in a book that says there are many *little things* that are really *big things*. As mentioned before, every good thing can have a bad side if it is over-emphasized. Therefore, I wanted to write a caution about that in both Chapters 37 and 38.

Our basic human nature tends to dwell on bad things and leave out the good things that God does for us. I remember something that Les Ollila taught many years ago, and it has it has stuck with me. Les called it "an attitude filter." He said that if a person has a bad attitude in any situation, the bad attitude will filter out all the good things so that all he can see are the bad things. If he has a good attitude, it will filter out all the bad things so that all he can see are the good things, and he can be content.

My daughter Gina gave me a good saying that illustrates this: "Bad attitude is like a flat tire. You can't get anywhere until you change it!"

In my extensive travels over the last 50 years or so, I have noticed this to be true. For instance, if a teacher or some students in a Christian school have a bad attitude, all they can see are the things they don't like about the school or church, and they will miss out on the blessings God wants them to have.

Let me give you a real situation with which I am familiar that will illustrate this. I personally know some people (I will not give any dates to protect the guilty) who came to Bob Jones University to teach, believing that it was in the will of God for them. However, after a short period of time they left the school because they did not care for the food in the Dining Common.

I like to satirically say that to me that is trying to have devotions out of a stolen Bible. They left the place to which God called them over an insignificant thing. Can you imagine a missionary who was called to the jungles of Africa doing that kind of thing? This is making a *big thing* out of something that should have been small in their eyes.

I am also thinking of a woman who came to me for counseling many years ago. In the counseling session all she did was criticize her husband: he was weak, he didn't understand her, and on and on. After listening to her for a long time, I finally told her that the problem was she had married this man of her own free will, and that according to God she had to submit to him in some of the areas where she was criticizing him.

I still remember vividly the day she came back for more help after one week. Her first words were: "I submitted to him all week and it didn't work!" I almost laughed in her face. I admonished her by saying: "You have been disobedient for many years, and you expect to fix it in a week?" That woman was making big things out of insignificant things that come to a married couple.

As a music teacher for about 70 years (I started teaching trombone when I was a teenager), I have known many aspiring musicians who have given up much too early because of the tedium of practice or because they missed a few notes in an early performances. A good musician is not one who makes no mistakes. It is one who keeps going and ignores the little mistakes that come in almost any performance.

Most preachers will tell you that their first sermons were not very good. They went home embarrassed about how poorly they communicated, or how quickly they ran out of the material they thought they had prepared. If they had given up at that point, God could never have used them in the way He wanted to.

The best example of *not* letting inconsequential things bother him was Joseph. He was somehow able to bring God into every situation he faced, and he did not let the distractions keep him from trusting the Lord. He brought God into the picture with Potiphar's wife, with the butler and baker in the prison, with Pharaoh, with his Egyptian wife and sons, with his doubting brothers, and with all the Israelites as he was about to die. This characteristic made him one of the few Bible characters against whom there is no record of stain, no matter what his outer circumstances were.

Perhaps we have come full circle in these two chapters. God wants us to know there are no *little decisions*, but he also wants us to not put too much emphasis on *insignificant things*. Let's ask Him to give us the wisdom to know the difference so that we can have good balance in our Christian lives.

Chapter 39

> ❧

OLD AGE IN THE BIBLE

Like me, you have probably wondered what happens to men and women in the Bible when they get old. Many of the ones that we admire because they were faithful to the Lord still suffered the ravages of time as they got older. God is teaching us that He is in control and that we must trust Him in every stage of our lives.

In fact, the Bible admonishes His people to give special honor to old men and women. Leviticus 19:32 says, "Thou shalt rise up [show respect] before the hoary head."

The first example of this is in Genesis 24:1 where the Scriptures say, "The Lord had blessed Abraham in all things." However, the beginning of that verse says that he "was old and well stricken in age." Henry Halley says that Abraham was "the greatest, purest, and most venerable of the patriarchs." Even though he had been able by God's grace to have a son at 99 years of age, he now bore all the signs that come to an old man.

The next example is Isaac in Genesis 37. Even though he probably lived quite a few years after this problem with Jacob and Esau, the Scripture informs us that he was old and "his eyes were dim, so that he could not see." Robert Jamieson says Isaac at this point was "a feeble, chronic invalid with a . . . taste for venison." He could have used one of his sheep, but he wanted his son to do what he could no longer do, hunt for a wild animal.

Another example is King David, who God said was a "man after His own heart" (1 Samuel 13:14). He still had weakness in his old age. Also 1 Kings 1:14 states that David was "old and stricken in years." Like other old people, even though his servants "covered him with clothes," they could not get him warm. The servants then convinced David to let them bring a "young virgin" to him to lie close to him to keep him warm.

Verse 4 of that chapter makes it clear that there was no immoral relationship between David and the young woman. It was the only thing the servants knew to do to try to preserve David's life in his old age. The words "knew her not" indicate that there was no sexual contact between them.

The old age and death of Moses is unique. Some commentaries say there is a possibility that God told Moses, since he is the author of the Pentateuch, about his own death that was to come. Deuteronomy 34:5-6 says, "So Moses, the servant of the LORD, died there in the land of Moab, according to the word of the LORD. And He [God] buried him in a valley in the land of Moab, over against Bethpeor; but no man knoweth of his sepulcher to this day."

Verse 9 of that same chapter says, "And Joshua, the son of Nun, was full of the spirit of wisdom; for Moses had laid his hands upon him. And the children of Israel hearkened unto him, and did as the

Lord commanded Moses." The account continues in the book of Joshua. Joshua 13:1-2 tells of Joshua when he was "old and stricken in years." In his case, God still had much work for him to do. That work covers ten chapters and about seven years.

Chapter 23 of the book of Joshua again mentions that "Joshua waxed old and stricken in age." However, he did not die until seventeen years later when he gave his final charge to the Israelites in Chapter 24. It is interesting to note that Joshua is credited there for burying the bones of Joseph that Moses brought with them when they left Egypt. It was 200 years after the death of Joseph that Moses carried his bones, but 262 years before they were buried at Shechem after Joshua took Moses' place in leading the Israelites.

There are three examples in the New Testament of people whom God used in their old age: Simeon and Anna, both mentioned in Chapter 2 of Luke. Both of them were just and devout in looking for the coming Messiah, and God kept them both alive until they had seen the child Jesus and could proclaim who He was.

The third example of the New Testament was the Apostle John, who was apparently an old man when he wrote the book of Revelation. Several things seem to indicate he was younger than Jesus at the time of the crucifixion (John 19:26-27). Assuming that he was in his twenties then, he still would be in his eighties when he was banished to the Isle of Patmos. God still used John as an old man to write the last book of the Bible—just as He had used Daniel as an old man to record His detailed prophecy of the four centuries between the Old and New Testaments (Daniel 11:2-35) and then write of the last years of the world and hints of the Glory to come.

Chapter 40

A FRUITFUL BOUGH

Grandma Campbell, my mother's mother, lived to be 75 years of age. One of her sayings as she approached old age was: "An old tree can bear fruit as well as a young one!" Grandma lived what she taught. She led many people to the Lord after she was "old and well-stricken in years."

Here is a poem she wrote two months before she went to be with her Lord:

Lord, teach me how to worship Thee in spirit and in truth;
Teach me how to wait on Thee, and thus renew my youth,
Teach me how to mount above the burdens of the day.
Lord, teach me, oh, please teach me how to let Thee have Thy way.

She was asking the Lord to still use her in her old age, and God granted her that request. I am, at my age of 87, still experiencing answers to some of the requests that my grandmother made for me many years ago. But let me relate an event that happened the Sunday after she passed away.

When the pastor of the church she was attending announced her passing the previous Tuesday, a lady in the back of the church stood up and said, "May I say something?" The pastor reluctantly agreed. Here is what the woman said: "I came to church today to thank her for leading me to Lord here last Sunday."

It is obvious that things must change as a person gets older: it takes longer to do things than it used to; it is difficult to remember things; things that seemed light before are difficult to lift; not everything works and what does work hurts; things that were easy to do are extremely difficult to do now; balance is a major problem and falling can easily become a problem; the blood doesn't circulate as it used to and the body is cold all the time; vision becomes blurred and it is easy to bump into things; reading labels and magazines is tiresome; spilling food on clothes is a common occurrence; the mind is like Swiss cheese, with holes in it; lack of hearing makes a person feel abandoned; and there are many other changes too numerous to mention.

However, it is still true that an old tree can still bear fruit. God has brought several things to my attention that let me know that He is not through with me just yet. Just last week God brought a young woman across my path that I met about four years ago. She is from Colombia, South America. When she was 12 years old, she heard one of my translated messages on the radio in Colombia and decided then that if she would ever be able to go to college, she would attend BJU because of what she heard me say on the radio.

Well, she came here four years ago to study nursing. Flora Jean and I met her then and took her to dinner several times. After two years, she had to go home to Ohio where her family now lives, so that she could save up money to come back to school. Last week as a senior nursing student, she visited the assisted living place where we now are, and she hugged me to thank me for being faithful so she could now find God's will for her life as a nurse. (See Chapter 52 for more information about this young woman.)

One more illustration! I received a call this week from one of my former students who is teaching others by means of modern technology. He is in Southern California and is teaching a young woman in Nebraska. As she received her master's degree recently, he told her she should obtain a copy of my book *Just Show Up: God Can Use You*. When she obtained a copy, she and her family read what Dr. John Vaughn had written about the Hidden Treasure Christian School for special needs children which he began in our church many years ago (Vignette #18, p. 91).

My former student titled an email he sent to me this week: "An Added Blessing of *Just Show Up*." This is just an unexpected extra addition to a project that the Lord helped me complete this year at the ripe old age of 87. The family is now seriously considering moving to Greenville to put her handicapped brothers in the school because they cannot find a good school that they would want to send them to in Nebraska. There is also a possibility that the young woman could teach in the school where her brothers would attend.

Chapter 41

"Keep Thy Heart"

In His Word, God has a lot to say about our hearts. If we have been saved for many years, we can gradually become accustomed to reading the words of Scripture without really taking to heart what they actually mean. They become *little things* to us. What God says about our hearts is one of those topics or issues.

For instance, the title I gave this chapter is from Proverbs 4:23. The key words in that chapter (see verses 5 and 7), revealing what God wants us to do, are *understanding* and *wisdom*. If we are going to be what God wants us to be, we must keep our *hearts*. I am not a Spanish scholar, but I must admit that I love the Spanish language for many reasons. One of the main reasons is the way the Reina-Valera version translates the Hebrew and the Greek.

As an example, Proverbs 4:23 in Spanish is "*Sobre toda cosa guardada, guarda tu corazón; Porque de él mana la vida*" (Above every guarded thing, guard your heart, because life flows from it). What that verse says is probably why God mentions the heart 830 times in His Word: 725 times in the Old Testament, and 105 times in the New Testament.

Some of my favorite Scriptures deal with music and the heart. For instance, Psalm 9:1 (addressed to the chief musician) says, "I will praise thee, O Lord, with my *whole heart*." Psalm 13:5b-6 says, "*My heart* shall rejoice in thy salvation. I will sing unto the Lord, because he hath dealt bountifully with me." Or consider Psalm 28:7: "*My heart* greatly rejoiceth; and with my song will I praise him." I also like what a black preacher once said to an atheist: "Psalm 14:1 says, 'The fool hath said in his *heart*, there is no God.' You're a big fool, you blabbed it out loud!"

Proverbs also has other verses about the heart, such as Proverbs 2:2: "Incline thine ear to wisdom, and apply thine *heart* to understanding." And Proverbs 3:3: "Let not mercy and truth forsake thee: bind them about thy neck; write them upon the table of thine *heart*." From the days of Ezra, on the first day of class for a Jewish child, the teacher would put honey over the Scripture on the child's slate, and have the child lick it. The idea was to have the Scripture become a part of the child's *heart* because it tasted so good.

This could be why Daniel "purposed in his *heart* that he would not defile himself" as a young captive in Babylon (Daniel 1:8). In Jerusalem between the ages of 6 and 10, like all Jewish boys of that time, he probably had memorized and hidden in his *heart* all five books of the Pentateuch: Genesis, Exodus, Leviticus, Numbers, and Deuteronomy. The truth of God was already ingrained in his *heart*.

It is also interesting to read the things God says about Lucifer in Isaiah 14:13. His basic problem that made him fall was that "he said in his *heart*" that he was going to take God off His throne and "be like the Most High." The devil's wicked *heart* caused him to have "I" trouble that shows up at least five times in that revealing passage of Isaiah.

The Lord Jesus summed up the matter of the *heart* in the Sermon on the Mount when He said, "Blessed are the pure in *heart*: for they shall see God" (Matthew 5:8). In that same sermon, the Master mind reader also said, "Where your treasure is, there will your *heart* be also" (Matthew 6:21). In another place, He said, "Out of the abundance of the *heart*, the mouth speaketh. A good man out of the good treasure of the *heart* bringeth forth good things" (Matthew 12:35-36). He also admonished the Pharisees that the greatest commandment is to "Love the Lord thy God, *with all thy heart*, and with all thy soul, and with all thy mind" (Matthew 22:37).

One of the clearest and most concise passages on how to be saved is found in Romans 10:9-10: "If thou shalt confess with thy mouth the Lord Jesus, and shalt believe in thine *heart* that God hath raised Him from the dead, thou shalt be saved. For with the *heart* man believeth unto righteousness, and with the mouth confession is made unto salvation." This is just another way of saying what the Lord said in the Sermon on the Mount: "Out of the abundance of the *heart*, the mouth speaketh."

We all should *take to heart* and apply what the Word of God says in every situation.

Chapter 42

THE REAL TEST

In the last chapter we talked about how important it is that we keep our hearts clean before God, because only He really knows our hearts. Jeremiah 17:9 makes this abundantly clear when it says, "The heart is deceitful above all things, and desperately wicked: *who can know it?*" Notice how strongly God admonishes us. And then in verse 10 he says, "I the LORD search the heart." God is interested in *little things*, and only He can know our hearts.

It is therefore only logical to assume that God is going to put us to the test when we glibly say to someone else or even to God Himself: "I love you with all my heart!" It is humbling to realize that our sovereign God who knows all about us takes it upon Himself to put us to the test to see if we genuinely mean business.

This is true when a person trusts Christ as his Savior. I have made it a practice over the years of my ministry to tell someone who has just trusted Christ that this test is coming! The Scripture that we often use in leading someone to the Lord is Romans 10:9-10. Without quoting the whole passage, let me point out and paraphrase what these verses say about the heart: If you believe *in your heart* . . . you will be saved . . . For *with the heart* man believes and becomes righteous.

It only makes sense that if God says we must believe *with the heart*, He will try our hearts to see if we meant business. There are several Scriptures that bear this out: 1 Chronicles 29:17, Jeremiah 11:20, Psalm 7:9, and Psalm 11:5. But the most forceful one is Proverbs 17:3, "The refining pot is for silver, and the furnace for gold: *but the LORD trieth the hearts*."

However, this is not only true at salvation; it is also true for the whole Christian life. God seeks to make us like His Son, and this is a life-long project. One verse in the significant eighth chapter of Romans makes this clear: "For whom he did foreknow, he also did predestinate to *be conformed to the image of His Son*" (Romans 8:29). Another verse expands on that principle when it says, "put on the new man, which is renewed in knowledge *after the image* of him that created him" (Colossians 3:19).

Let me give several examples of how God has tested me. The first one that comes to mind is when I wanted to serve God as a teenager. I thought that meant that I had to become a pastor, and the generous woman who paid my way through college thought that was what I was going to do. When I realized God wanted me to serve Him through music, I had a decision to make. Do I do what my benefactor wanted, or do I do what I believe the Lord wants me to do? By the way, the woman never repeated what she did for me for anyone else because she thought she made a mistake in helping me.

God put me to the test right after I graduated from college. Was I following what my heart said or what my emotions said? I decided to go to His Word and search. When I was looking in my Bible for something else, I came across 1 Chronicles 9:33, which says, "These are the singers [musicians], chief of the fathers of the Levites, who *remaining in the chambers were free*: for they were employed in that work *day and night.*" Not in an audible voice, but God through His Word just said to me: "Are you going to obey me and do what I want you to do, or not?" As soon as I said "yes," God began to open musical opportunities for me in serving Him, and He has continued to do so for almost 70 years.

As I mentioned earlier, I have probably had more opportunities to preach than most pastors ever have. There have been weeks when I had a very busy schedule and preached at least fifteen times that week. That would be in addition to the large Sunday school class that I taught every Lord's Day morning.

The next test that God brings to my mind was when Flora Jean and I were facing a terrific problem that I will not delineate here. We had been married for almost 25 years, the church that we served was thriving, Majesty Music was growing and expanding, my speaking schedule was taking me all over the world, and the Lord was seeming to bless all that we were doing for Him. That is when the test came!

Without giving any details, I want to tell you what we did. We knelt down by our couch, heartbroken and crying, and here is what we said to our Heavenly Father: "Lord, we have claimed your promises about this situation (and we quoted the verses we were claiming), but it appears they are not being fulfilled. But, Lord, we are trusting You, and we are still going to serve You, even if we never see the fulfillment of those promises." I must admit, God did not change our circumstances; He changed our hearts! He was putting our hearts to the test to see if we really meant business.

One of the most frightening tests I have ever had was when I was in Haiti to speak there in January of 2010. On Tuesday afternoon at 4:53, the 7.0 magnitude earthquake suddenly struck. If the house I was standing near had collapsed, I would have been killed. A three-story house right across the dirt street was flattened, and a school close by with 200 students collapsed, killing all but four of the students. I wrote a book about this experience that is still available from Majesty Music. It is called *Haiti: A Time for Miracles*, and it reveals all the things the Lord did to protect me.

An interesting sidelight is how my daughter, Shelly, was doing everything she could to get me off the island. When the family did not know for four days whether or not I was alive, Shelly was particularly concerned. On the Friday after the earthquake struck, she spent most of the day (at least 13 hours) trying to contact the published information number in Washington, D.C., to see if she could get any information and help. At about 8 p.m., she got through. When the woman who answered the phone asked why Shelly was calling, and Shelly gave her my name, the woman said, "Is he a musician?" When Shelly said "Yes," the woman said, "I know him!"

The helpful woman who answered the phone is Lisa Pittman of the U.S. Embassy in Hong Kong. She was home on vacation and had volunteered to help take calls in Washington because so many people were concerned about Americans in Haiti during the earthquake. She knew us because when our son, Randy, was in Hong Kong, she had been a help to him. You may believe that was a coincidence, but I don't!

In what I am going to write now, I could be misunderstood, but I am going to write it anyway. In our sixty-six years of marriage, I have told Flora Jean many, many times that I love her *with all my heart.* And I mean it sincerely! However, God is allowing my heart to go through the biggest test of my life. Flora Jean has advanced dementia and her short-term memory is basically gone. She is also becoming physically weak and although I try to have her do simple exercises, it is almost impossible. If anyone reading this has gone through what I am talking about, you will understand when I say it is like living with a child. However, you need not try to correct things as you would with a child. It does absolutely no good with an adult.

Let me state what I believe God is trying to teach me at this point in my life. Here is the principle: "When you do something *with your heart,* you must not expect the other person to do anything for you!" When your mate cannot even understand or remember what you are doing for him or her, you are being taught by God and it tries your heart. You can get the problem settled one day, but then it comes back again the next day or sooner.

I remember a man who was asked by a friend why he spent so much time with his wife of many years when she did not even know who he was. His reply was: "I still know who she is!" That is a heart of love! I must admit that I am still growing in that area of my life. I usually do well with the *big things*, but it is often with the *little things* that I fail. God is still testing my heart to see if I am real.

Chapter 43

GOD USES ORDINARY PEOPLE

God knows the value of ordinary people because He made so many of them! 1 Corinthians 1:26 makes this clear when it says, "Not many wise, not many mighty, not many noble are called." Verse 29 goes on to give the reason: "that no flesh should glory in His presence."

The Bible mentions several people who were ordinary little people yet were important in situations. 2 Samuel 23:8-39 tells of David's friends who are called "mighty men." I doubt that there are very many Bible students who could name any of those men without other clues being given.

Here are the names of three rather ordinary men who brought essential supplies to King David in the wilderness when Absalom had rebelled against him (2 Samuel 17:27):

- Shobi—A gracious man who came from a pagan family and helped David in a time of need

- Machir—A grateful man who protected a helpless boy, Mephibosheth, thus repaying a debt of love (2 Samuel 9:3-4)

- Barzilla—A godly old man who later refused to be rewarded by David and "returned to his own place" (2 Samuel 19:31-39)

One of the best examples of the ordinary people principle is Abraham's servant in Genesis 24. This unbelievably wise and faithful servant is never named in that chapter; he never prayed for himself; led by God, he went to the right place at the right time with the right message; he was never rewarded for what he did; and he was content to be a servant the rest of his life. That is why my autobiography is called *I Being in the Way, the Lord Led Me.* I want to be the kind of servant that ordinary faithful man was.

Quite often in Scripture the ordinary person is only mentioned in passing so that we miss the significance of what that person did. This is true in Ruth 1:6 where we learn that Naomi "arose with her daughters in law, that she might return from the country of Moab." Then comes the reason: *"for she had heard that the LORD had visited his people in giving them bread."* This message from an unnamed ordinary person caused Naomi, along with Ruth, to go to Bethlehem-Judah to receive the blessings of God that awaited them there.

An additional Biblical illustration is the story of the widow of Zarephath, another unnamed person whom God chose and commanded to sustain His prophet (1 Kings 17:8-16). When Elijah asked the widow for water and then "a morsel of bread," she responded that she had only enough for her and her son to eat, and die. When she did as Elijah asked, "the barrel of meal wasted not, neither did the cruse of oil fail" until the Lord sent rain as He had promised. The widow's obedience gave her provisions far exceeding anything she could possibly have expected.

On one of our trips to Jerusalem, I was given a *little thing* that I treasure. It is called "the widow's mite," and it is mentioned in Mark 12:41-44 and Luke 21:1-4. It was actually two mites, but the coin I was given is supposed to be the very kind the widow would have used. Again, like other "ordinary little people," this widow is never named. However, her generosity with what she gave out of her poverty was commended by the Lord Himself and is still remembered after 2,000 years. I have this coin with a stone from the Wailing Wall in my keepsakes to remind me to be generous with what the Lord gives me.

For our next example we will use a man who is named, but one of whom we know very little. In fact, if you mention his name in most churches today, no one will have any idea who he was. The Apostle Paul said that he was "my brother, and companion in labor, and fellow soldier, but your messenger, and he that ministered to my wants." Paul then goes on to say, "Receive him therefore in the Lord with all gladness; and hold such in reputation: Because for the work of Christ he was nigh unto death, not regarding his life, to supply your lack of service toward me."

Have you guessed who this outstanding servant of the Lord was? He is mentioned only twice, and both references to him are in the same book of the Bible. The book is Philippians, and his name is Epaphroditus (Philippians 2:25-30 and 4:18). You may have trouble pronouncing his name, let alone knowing who he was. Here was an ordinary man that God used in a great way to help the Apostle Paul do the work that God called him to do.

For our last illustration, we will look at a group of men whose names we do not know. For background, you need to know to whom the Apostle Paul was chained to on his trip to Rome: the Praetorian Guard. These elite soldiers were part of Caesar's most-trusted legion. The ones mentioned were centurions, but they were Paul's "captive audience" because Paul was not only chained to them; they were chained to him! Many of them must have complained about being assigned to guard one Jewish man, a *little thing*.

But if you have studied and *know* the apostle Paul, you know that he must have witnessed to each of those men and won many of them to the Lord. At least, each soldier must have heard this Roman citizen witness to others, or pray and sing praises to God. The book of Philippians reveals two places where Paul mentions these men. In Philippians 1:13 Paul says: "My bonds in Christ are manifest in all the palace" (Caesar's court). Verse 14 seems to imply that many of these men ("the brethren in the Lord") became confident and bold "to speak the word without fear."

Then in Philippians 4:22, Paul says: "All the *saints* salute you, chiefly they that are of Caesar's household" (his Imperial Civil Service). This elite group had members all over the world at that time. They were palace officials, secretaries, and others who conducted the affairs of the Roman Empire, and the Apostle Paul called them *saints*. It is not exaggerating to say that many of these men must have been led to Christ for Paul to call them saints! This is just another example of unnamed people being used of God to spread the gospel to the then-known world.

Chapter 44

FULL CIRCLE

As I am writing this, Flora Jean and I are living in an assisted living facility called Shepherd's Care Center. The extended care insurance policy that we took out twenty years ago was actually two policies although I did not realize it: one policy for me and another one for her.

Three years ago, as Flora Jean began to lose her short-term memory, the insurance would have paid for her to come here, but they would not pay for me. I think the easiest way to say it is that even though I was already in my eighties three years ago, I could still think and care for myself, and that left me unqualified. I promised Flora Jean, even before that time, that since she has followed me around to fifty countries, I would never allow her to go to a place like this without me. We stay together until the Lord takes one of us home, or better yet, if He comes to get us.

We came here eight weeks ago when the insurance decided to pay for me. The journey is very interesting, especially for Flora Jean, who has trouble understanding what is going on: Why are we here? When are we going home? When do we get a truck to move the furniture? Why do these people [the workers] keep coming in this room? Where is the kitchen so I can cook? And so on. I believe the

Lord has worked for us in putting us here, but it is very difficult to explain that to Flora Jean.

I cannot get my mind off the fact that the Lord brought us, and particularly me, full circle. If you have read my autobiography, you know that I grew up in a very poor family with few resources. That is where we are now. The insurance is paying for us to be here, but the only money we have for ourselves is what we get from Social Security (what a misnomer!). By the time we pay for our medicines (one of Flora Jean's is over $6,000 a year), even the government considers us to be in the lower poverty level.

However, that is not the purpose of this chapter of this book. The Lord is reminding me of what I believe I have known for the last 87 years: I am nobody special! I am just one of the ordinary people! Anything good that has come out of my life and ministry has ALL been of God, and not me. I do not deserve any special attention.

There have been a number of outstanding servants of the Lord who have stayed here, but most of the residents and the people who work here are ordinary people. I am not known as "Dr. Garlock" here. I am either Mr. or just Frank depending on the speaker. I am not on a special diet as some of the residents are, so I just eat the same thing that most of the residents get. I am awakened at 5:30 each morning to take the medicine they believe is necessary. I need to check out and back in every time I leave the facility. In some ways, it is like being a student at BJU again.

I believe what the Lord is showing me is that He still wants to use me "in whatsoever state I am" and "therewith to be content"

(Philippians 4:11). The majority of the people working here are at the low end of the pay scale. They work here either because they are poor or because they love helping older people. It is amazing to watch them give care to people who need special attention. It is also amazing to watch them respond kindly to residents who *demand* special attention and sometimes say unkind things to them.

This has given me a renewed appreciation for ordinary people. In fact, when I realized that some of the workers are probably working for less money than we receive from Social Security, I gave some of what we receive to as many of them as I could as a Christmas gift. The appreciation I received was overwhelming.

The Lord is also teaching me that He is not through with me yet. There are still many things that I need to learn. One thing is patience. I am still embarrassed to admit that I have tremendous patience for some things and no patience for other things. When we went to Shelly's house about ten miles away the other day, Flora Jean asked me the same question every two minutes for the whole trip as we were going. I tried not to show any impatience as I answered each time.

I am delighted that the Lord has kept us together for 66 years and that we still have genuine love for each other that is obvious to all who are around us. I have *no regrets* for having served the Lord side by side and hand in hand with God's choice for all these years. I remind Flora Jean of what her parents used to say when they visited us and they saw how much love we showed to each other. Her parents would say, "Are you like this all the time?" To which we would reply, "You should see us when you are not here!"

Chapter 45

> ❦

A Cup of Water

One of the most potent exemplifications of *little things* in the Bible is how often God, almost insignificantly, mentions something that we skip over because we do not think it is important.

It is meaningful for us to note one *little thing* that is mentioned only in the book of Mark and not in the other three Gospels. It may be because Mark's purpose in writing his account of the life of Christ was to show the servant character of our Savior. That is probably why Mark dwells on the *deeds* and not on the *words* of our Lord. He also points out how often Christ talked about deeds. Here is one of those portentous statements of our Savior.

> *For whosoever shall give you a cup of water to drink in my name, because ye belong to Christ, verily I say unto you, he shall not lose his reward* (Mark 9:41).

We all have a tendency to do well on the big things we do and the big problems we face. At the same time, some *little thing* or problem comes our way and we absolutely fail to do what we should. I have personally gotten upset with myself, and even mad at myself sometimes. That is because after I have taken care of a big problem successfully, I almost immediately fail in responding to a small problem that came my way.

Our Lord must have been very much aware that we would have this tendency in our lives, and he used Mark to point out several instances where a *little thing*, like a cup of water done in His name, can make a tremendous difference in someone else's life.

Mark emphasizes some *little things* in his account of the Gospel: how we treat little children (10:13-16); what we do with any "riches" that God allows us to have (10:23-31); real servanthood (10:35-45); the power of faith (11:22-24); forgiveness (11:25-26); the widow's mite (12:41-44); deceitful prophets (13:6); watchfulness (13:34-37); doing what we can (14:8); holding our peace (14:61); and Simon bearing the Lord's cross (15:21).

I have written a book of vignettes that is a series of *little things* that have happened in my own life. At the time of these events they seemed like *little things*, and many of them I did not hear about until many years after they occurred (39 years later, 43 years later, etc.). In fact, I called the book *Just Show Up: God Can Use You* because I believe God can use anyone who strives to know God personally. I always remember what Jerome Hines, the famous opera singer said: "People say I believe in God. No! I know Him!" When a person is full of God, his aroma will flood into the lives of others.

Again, in reading back over the book to see what the people who wrote the vignettes said, what I did was really very small. However, for the person involved, it was *big thing*. (Vignettes #6, 16, 18, and 28 all reveal this.) The next chapter describes another example: what a missionary to Mexico did many years ago reaped results that he probably never expected and probably never heard about.

A "cup of water given in His name" can reap eternal results that we more than likely will never hear about until Christ gives out the rewards in heaven.

Chapter 46

THE POWER OF THE GOSPEL

I heard this testimony in 1996 on my first trip to Monterrey, Mexico, to encourage the people there to realize that UCLA (La Universidad de las Americas) could someday become a reality. This testimony was given by Pastor David Cortes at a Leadership Conference to show the people there what God can do when we trust Him. This university that ministers to college students from five countries is a testimony of God's love and mercy as well. Here is my feeble translation of what Pastor Cortes said that day, more than 20 years ago.

TESTIMONY OF DAVID CORTES

Many years ago, a missionary came to the village where I was born. He came before I was born and who he was and how he came to be there, I do not know. My father died more than twenty years ago and my mother does not remember, since the missionary knocked on the door soon after they were married.

Of all the people in the village, Mama and Papa were the only ones converted that day when the missionary came to our town. But they gave themselves to the Lord and embraced the things of God with all their hearts and with all their strength.

They purposed to raise a new generation for the glory of the Lord when my oldest brother and the other eleven children were born.

I am the fourth and there are eight younger than I am, but my Papa and Mama dedicated themselves to teach us every day in the Word of God. We did this every day! At a family altar every day! And now, of the twelve, nine are involved in the full-time work of the Lord. Five are pastors, and my four sisters are married to pastors. That means that there are nine of us serving the Lord full-time.

I don't know where that missionary is who came to the door of our house and I never have met him. He could not have known all the results that were going to come as a result of that missionary visit. Papa brought many souls to Christ. When we were small, Papa would take us back to the villages and the places where he used to sing as a mariachi before he was converted.

As I am one of the oldest, I remember with more clarity than my younger brothers and sisters. When my father showed Christian films on the largest walls of the buildings in the cities where we would go, he also preached the gospel of Jesus Christ. He did this in the places where he had been before, singing songs as he had done in his earlier life, but this time he was singing for the Lord.

All those souls who were brought to Christ came through the testimony of my father. All the souls that my brothers and sisters and our ministries have won by the grace of God, are on account of that unknown missionary who came to our little town.

Many times I have given thanks to God for him. I believe he stands in the presence of the Lord. Many times when some large thing happens in my life, when I complete another year, or another blessing comes to our church, I remember that missionary and give thanks for him. I don't know who he is, but I know I will meet him in heaven, and I will give thanks to the Lord for him.

It is very possible that that missionary went away wondering if this young couple really had found Christ, or if they were just "making a profession" to get rid of him. In addition to that, there was no one in that little town to teach them about the Lord since they were the only ones who trusted Christ while that missionary was there knocking on doors.

Only eternity will reveal the results of the faithfulness of that unknown missionary in the lives of the thousands who have been saved and gone on to serve the Lord. All of this is because one day a nameless missionary knocked on the door of a tiny Mexican home in a little town and led a young couple to Christ. May the Lord help each one of us to use every opportunity He gives us to witness for our Savior. We may never see the results here on this earth. We may have to wait until heaven to learn how God used us for His glory, especially in the little places.

Chapter 47

Our Little World

The secular ungodly world cannot understand why God would take the interest in the earth that the Bible reveals He does. Because the *little thing*, the globe on which we exist, is so tiny in comparison to the expansive universe that we know exists, worldly science believes that there must be other earths just like ours far out in space.

This is just another example of how man's knowledge and understanding is so far from the truth because they leave the Bible out of their thinking. There are many things in the Bible that point to the fact that the globe on which we exist is unique. That is because God has created it to be that way. The Word of God declares that the earth exists along with the sun, the moon, and even all the stars as a habitation for mankind, who is the pinnacle of God's creation.

This is just one reason that God gave us the book of Genesis in the Bible. It is so encouraging to realize that there are organizations like the Institute for Creation Research, Answers in Genesis (the Creation Museum, the Ark Encounter), and the Museum of the Bible—organizations that place a strong emphasis on what Genesis teaches about the earth and the universe that our almighty sovereign God has created for us.

J. S. Bach, like many outstanding composers down through the centuries, emphasized what is called a "conservation of *means*." In other words, good composers do not add anything to the music that does not contribute to the purpose for which they are composing. The Holy Spirit, who guided all the writers of Scripture, is the Master Composer of a "conservation of *words*" to emphasize what He wants man to know.

For instance, in just five verses and 63 words in the Hebrew language, the Third Person of the Trinity told us exactly what *They*, and I use that word intentionally (*Elohim*), did in creating the firmament (Genesis 1:14-18). In Scripture the Hebrew word translated as *firmament* denotes an expanse, a wide extent.

Here is a simple short outline of what those verses say about the purpose of the whole firmament:

- For day and night
- For signs and seasons
- For days and years
- For light upon the earth
- Almost humorously, God adds that "He made the stars also"!

Our great God was so interested in this little tiny earth that He, and only He could do it, made the whole universe to meet the needs of mankind. Even more mind-boggling than that, He takes a special interest in each one of us, who are so miniscule that we are an insignificant speck of dust on the globe. It is also enlightening to find that scientists have discovered that stars vibrate in a way that is analogous to the vibrations that we hear as sounds. In the 1960s Caltech physicist Robert Leighton discovered the five-minute oscillation on the surface of the sun. Put in terms of sound, that would be a super-bass note sixteen octaves below middle C. Perhaps in eternity we will be able to hear the morning stars singing together (Job 38:7)!

For instance, the psalmist says,

> *When I consider thy heavens, the work of thy fingers, the moon and the stars, which thou hast ordained; what is man, that thou art mindful of him? and the son of man that thou visitest [carest for] him? For thou hast made him a little lower than the angels, and hast crowned him with glory and honor. Thou madest him to have dominion over the works of thy hands; thou hast put all things under his feet* (Psalm 8:3-6).

How much clearer does God need to be in revealing His purpose in making the Universe? Our great God spoke the Universe into existence with the purpose of taking care of the needs of His crowning creation, human beings. This ought to fill our hearts with overwhelming joy as we contemplate what our wonderful sovereign God has done for us insignificant beings, *little things*.

I can't help thinking of a little song I wrote in 1983 for the "Patch the Pirate" series after hearing a sermon by my friend, Dr. Bob Taylor, on the greatness of our God:

> *He's so great and I'm so small;*
> *Jesus holds me lest I fall.*
> *He's the Ruler over all—*
> *He's so great and I'm so small.*

A whole book could be written on what I have touched on briefly here, but most of you who read this will get the point.

Chapter 48

WISER IN THEIR GENERATION

This will probably be the longest chapter in this book because of the nature of the subject. I am thinking of what Jesus said in Luke 16:8: "The children of this world are wiser in their generation than the children of light." The best exegesis of this verse that I have ever seen is by David Brown in the commentary that contains his name. Here are a few phrases from that commentary that help explain what Jesus was teaching: [the children of this world] "are wiser *for* their own generation," [they] "have their portion in this life," and "with what untiring energy, determination, and perseverance they prosecute their purposes [we should] turn to our own advantage [that] which they shamefully abuse."[1]

Have you ever noticed how this is true in the political world? The liberals never give up! They don't get what they want the first time, so they keep coming back for it. Quite often, they just come at it a different way. They didn't get the Supreme Court to give them abortion the first time they asked for it, so they kept coming back. Various anti-abortion laws have been in force in each state since at least 1900. The conservatives don't seem to have learned this. They

---

1 The Jamieson-Fausset-Brown Bible Commentary, pp. 292-293.

give up too easily, and let the liberals have their way. This is also true for us Christians. We witness to someone and they refuse, and so we give up. I think this is a part of what Jesus was saying: learn from "the children of this world." They are wiser "in their generation" than the children of light.

I have always wondered how we who know the Lord and have the Holy Spirit to guide us could possibly be less wise than the world is. However, what the Lord is saying is that we should have the same energy, determination, and perseverance that the children of the world have, but we should be displaying those characteristics because we want God's will for our lives. In that same light, it is amazing how often unsaved people understand things that Christians refuse to see. The best musical example that I can think of for this conundrum is when the world says rock music is bad, but some Christians say it is not as bad as the world says it is. That is why they think they can use it for the Lord.

This type of thing seems to happen quite often in science. Although many scientific things have been discovered by Christians, unsaved scientists have made discoveries too. Here is a long incredible quotation by an avowed agnostic:[1]

> Has anyone provided proof of God's inexistence? Not even close. Has quantum cosmology explained the emergence of the universe or why it is here? Not even close. Have our sciences explained why our universe seems to be fine-tuned to

---

1 The Devil's Delusion: Atheism and Its Scientific Pretensions by David Berlinski. To find this scientist's credentials, put his name into Google and read what comes up.

allow for the existence of life? Not even close. Are physicists and biologists willing to believe in anything so long as it is not religious thought? Close enough. Has rationalism and moral thought provided us with an understanding of what is good, what is right, and what is moral? Not close enough. Has secularism in the terrible 20th century been a force for good? Not even close, to being close. Is there a narrow and oppressive orthodoxy in the sciences? Close enough. Does anything in the sciences or their philosophy justify the claim that religious belief is irrational? Not even in the ball park. Is scientific atheism a frivolous exercise in intellectual contempt? Dead on.

If moral statements are about something, then the universe is not quite as science suggests it is, since physical theories, having said nothing about God, say nothing about right or wrong, good or bad. To admit this would force philosophers to confront the possibility that the physical sciences offer a grossly inadequate view of reality. And since philosophers very much wish to think of themselves as scientists, this would offer them an unattractive choice between changing their allegiances [and] accepting their irrelevance.

Here are some quotations from another scientific magazine.[2]

Earth is one special planet. It has liquid water, plate tectonics, and an atmosphere that shelters it from the worst of the

---

2 "What Makes Earth Special Compared to Other Planets," Space.com/5595-earth-special-compared-planets.html July 8, 2006

sun's rays. But many scientists agree our planet's most special feature might just be us. It's the only planet we know of that has life.

The fact that Earth hosts not just life, but intelligent life, makes it doubly unique ... To enable life, this most special of attributes, planet Earth has a number of ideal features ... The Earth is remarkable in its precisely-tuned amount of water, not too much to cover the mountains, and not so little that it's a dry desert.

Our planet's Goldilocks-like "just right" location in the solar system keeps the earth from freezing or burning up. The distance from the sun is precise. Another "just-right" aspect of earth is its size: If it was much smaller, it wouldn't be able to hold on to our precious atmosphere; much larger and it might be a gas giant too hot for life.

The earth's own magnetic field protects it from solar winds among other things. It is incredibly fast, spinning around the sun at 67,000 miles per hour, but we don't feel it moving, because its speed is constant. Any changes could destroy the earth and us with it.

Jupiter acts like a giant moon that blocks debris from striking the earth. Our [own] moon stabilizes the earth's rotation, helps life and pulls the ocean's tides. Any other place in our solar system, you would not want to be!

Even "The Weather Channel" recognizes what a wonderful place God has made for us. Just a few paragraphs from their website reveal several wonders of the world that God has made for us.

> For those who missed out on "Secrets of the Earth," it explores our planet with the same sense of awe and wonder normally reserved for alien worlds. Computer graphics, visual analogies and expert scientists combine to reveal amazing, little-known aspects of the world, from canyons of gravity that warp space and time to rain triggered by cosmic rays.

> [Alaska is] home to 17 of America's 20 tallest peaks, 80 percent of the country's active volcanoes, and has more active glaciers than the rest of the inhabited world. Scale the highest peak in North America, explore mysterious ice caves, and witness the thunderous collapse of glaciers where the ice meets the sea.

> Fortunately, the real world does hold a number of mysterious and spectacular sights, from caves in Mexico filled with giant crystals to manmade palaces spread across the world. There are still plenty of hiding places beneath the surface.

> And then there are the Chocolate Hills of the Philippines. The hundreds of mysterious mounds are around 160 feet tall and are almost symmetrical and covered with grass. Despite how perfectly formed they seem, the mounds aren't manmade and scientists are unsure about their origins.

From forests full of giant trees to jagged mountain peaks, America's national parks offer visitors an opportunity to experience beautiful landscapes and natural wonders all year round.

These scientists recognize what the Bible has always taught. God is interested in *little things* as well as huge things, and He made the world, the moon, the solar system, and all the stars for His greatest creation, mankind. He gave us His Word to reveal that to those who seek the truth, and we should never apologize or back down from proclaiming what the Bible teaches, especially the *little things*. If the world is that wise, how much wiser should we Christians be?

INTERLUDE: THE LENS OF GOD

The last four chapters of this book are going to be about things that I would like to call miracles. However, I know cannot call these things "miracles" since they do not fit the classic definition of that word. Therefore, I am calling these four chapters "The Lens of God." The concept comes from what my daughter, Gina, wrote for *Just Show Up: God Can Use You*. The explanation of that concept is: Don't look through the *lens of circumstances* to understand God; look through the *lens of God* to understand circumstances.

Following the pattern of alternating Bible illustrations with personal ones, Chapter 49 will be Old Testament illustrations, Chapter 50 will be past events, Chapter 51 will be New Testament illustrations, and Chapter 52 will be current events. There is a thread that runs through the Bible that ties all of the recorded events together, and I have tried to do the same thing with this book. The Bible thread is centered on the person and divinity of Christ, the Old Testament looking forward to it, and the New Testament looking back at it. The thread of this book is the wonderful, Almighty God, who controls everything for those who know and trust Him to lead and guide them.

These last four chapters are particularly written for readers, like some that I have known, who like to read the end of a book before they finish the rest of the book. I hope that these chapters will inspire that type of reader to go back and read the rest of the book. For an excellent illustration of the principle of the *lens of God* that is in these chapters, read Vignette #33, pages 171-176 of *Just Show Up: God Can Use You*.

Chapter 49

CONTRASTS

I title this chapter "Contrasts" because the two main people I want to mention demonstrate the contrast between the mindset and heart of a father and a son. In the lives and experiences of these two men, God is showing how their individual views of God seem to determine so much of what happens in their lives. The father appears to always view God through *the lens of his circumstances* and the son views his circumstances through *the lens of God*.

Let's begin with the father: Jacob. He eventually became a "prince with God," but it took him almost all of his life to get there. The first we hear of him in Scripture is in chapter twenty-five of Genesis where we learn that he was the younger of twins, a "mama's boy," and completely different from Esau, his older brother, whose heel he grabbed with his hand as he was being born (Genesis 25:26). We also learn there that he was cunning so that he talked Esau into selling to him for some pottage (broth or soup) the birthright that the older brother should have had.

This is the first indication of Jacob's believing that he needed to take matters into his own hands because God had allowed Esau to be born before he was. He was looking at life through *the lens of circumstances* instead of *the lens of God*.

The next time we hear of Jacob is in chapter 27 of Genesis when he believes, along with his mother, that he has to trick his father Isaac out of the birthright. He connives in many ways because Isaac falsely believes he might die soon since he is going blind. Isaac does give him a blessing, but it is not the one Jacob wanted. Let's look at what Isaac actually gave him:

> *God give thee of the dew of heaven, and the fatness of the earth, and plenty of corn and wine: Let people serve thee, and nations bow down to thee: be lord over thy brethren, and let thy mother's sons bow down to thee: cursed be every one that curseth thee, and blest every one that blesseth thee* (Genesis 27:28-29).

That is the whole blessing that Jacob received at that time! For some reason, which is typical of those who are trying to deceive others, they themselves become deceived. Jacob did not really get the blessing he was seeking. We need to look at Genesis 28 to find that.

> *God Almighty (El Shaddai) bless thee, and make thee fruitful, and multiply thee, that thou mayest be a multitude of people;* ***and give thee the blessing of Abraham, to thee, and to thy seed with thee****; that thou mayest inherit the land wherein thou art a stranger, which God gave* ***to Abraham*** (Genesis 28:3-4).

It appears obvious that God intended to give **the blessing of Abraham** to Jacob if he had been looking through *the lens of God* instead of *the lens of circumstances*. He did not need to try to trick

Isaac to get it. It is also enlightening to read later about how his uncle Laban was a better trickster than Jacob was so that Jacob was treated "in kind" for every trick in which he tried to deceive Isaac (Genesis 29-30).

If we skip over to chapters 42 and 43 of Genesis, we then learn that Jacob is still looking at God through *the lens of circumstances.* Joseph has kept Simeon in Egypt to be certain the brothers would come back, and he has strongly charged the brothers to bring their younger brother with them when they come. Joseph knew they would be coming back because the famine was not over. When Jacob and the brothers see the money that "the man" (Joseph) put in their sacks of grain, Jacob is afraid and says:

> *Me have ye bereaved of my children: Joseph is not, and Simeon is not, and ye will take Benjamin away:* **all these things are against me** (Genesis 42:36).

He still does not trust God enough to realize that God is working all those things together for his good (Romans 8:28).

Let's contrast that with his son Joseph's *lens of God.* Having arrived in Egypt as a slave after being sold by his brothers, we find him trusting God for the next 11 chapters of this great book of the Bible (over one fifth of the book of Genesis). In fact, Joseph mentions God at least 23 times and in every circumstance that he finds himself in: with Potiphar's wife, with the butler and baker, with Pharaoh, in naming his sons, to his brothers when they come to Egypt to buy grain, when he reveals himself to his brothers, after Jacob dies, and when he himself is about to die.

Our natural instinct would be to think that the older person would be the strong one. However, as it is in another illustration that I want to mention once more, it is the younger one who has the correct lens and is looking at circumstances as God sees them. That illustration is the contrast between Naomi and Ruth in the book that bears her name.

Elimelech and Naomi have left Bethlehem-Judah because they were focusing on the circumstances there. After the father and the two sons have died in Moab, Naomi hears that the circumstances in Bethlehem-Judah have improved. So she starts out to go back home with the two daughters-in-law, Orpah and Ruth. Orpah is persuaded by her mother-in-law to go back to Moab, but not Ruth!

We have no idea where Ruth got the desire to follow whatever light she had received from her backslidden mother-in-law, but *the lens of God* she displays in verse 16 of chapter one of this book is amazing. It reveals a basic principle of the Word of God: **if we follow whatever light God has shown us, no matter how small, He will then reveal the next step He wants us to take.** So often, we want the Lord to show us the future before we step out, but God seldom reveals that to us. We must obey what He has shown us before He reveals His will for the future!

Notice again that it is the younger person who has *the lens of God* and refuses to retreat and go back from following what God has revealed to her. There was no way Ruth could have known all that was in store for her in Bethlehem-Judah or all the wonderful plans God had designed for any person, many years later, who would follow her

example of submission that is still repeated in weddings to this day
(Ruth 1:16-17).

These "contrasts" that God has revealed to us in His Word are definitely not *little things*, or He would not have put them there. As with
every other illustration that our loving Lord has revealed to us, may
we learn to look at life (the circumstances) through *the lens of God* so
that we can respond just as both Joseph and Ruth did.

Chapter 50

ACCORDING TO HIS PURPOSE

Whenever things happen that we do not understand, it is essential that we make sure to recognize that God is in control, and that His sovereign purpose is working out. We, in spite of our human frailty, must seek to determine how God is viewing the situation and how He can make everything work out for our good if we really love Him.

I must admit that I am embarrassed that there have been times that my loving Lord has had to bring me to the end of myself before I would admit that I was facing a situation where I had absolutely no answers. It seems that at those times I believe that if I work hard enough and long enough, I can make things work out the way I want them to. There have been times that I even found myself asking the Lord to follow my plan. As someone has said, "If you want to hear God laugh, tell Him your plans."

Or as the famous Scotch poet Bobby Burns wrote, "*O wad some Power the giftie gie us. To see oursels as ithers see us! It wad frae mony a blunder free us.*" In our English, that would be: "Oh, would some Power the rare gift give us, to see ourselves as others see us! It would from many a blunder free us!" Burns also wrote: "*The best laid schemes o' Mice an' Men gang aft agley* [go oft awry]."[1]

The main event I want to write about in this chapter is my experience of being on the "fourth-world" island of Haiti when the devastating 7.0 magnitude earthquake hit at 4:53 p.m. on January 12, 2010. There were two aftershocks of 5.9 and 5.5 magnitude, and I experienced them all. I mentioned this event incidentally in Chapter 42 of this book, but I want to discuss what I believe was the main purpose of all the Lord did for me in getting me out of Haiti after the earthquake struck.

My natural instinct was to wonder why I did not get to do what I thought was the main purpose in my going to the island of Haiti. It wasn't until I arrived back in Greenville, South Carolina, that I realized how God was working. That purpose was not mainly in the miraculous things the Lord did to keep me alive and get me back home.

The homecoming of missionary Sarah Bennett and me were the opportunities that the Lord gave both of us. I might add that the Lord gave that opportunity to the rest of our family as well. He opened the door to give testimonies of the grace of the Lord that we never could have had any other way. All the major TV networks, a large number of newspapers including the *Greenville News*, and thousands of people all over the world heard our testimonies.

---

1 "To a Louse, on seeing one on a lady's bonnet at church in 1776."

If we had asked the news networks to give us time to tell of God's goodness under ordinary circumstances, we would have gotten no-where. Because of the two of us being there for that earthquake, God gave us many, many opportunities that never could have come any other way. I wrote a book about this experience that is still available from Majesty Music. It is called *Haiti: A Time for Miracles*, and it reveals all the things the Lord did to protect me.

One event that particularly stands out in my mind is the CBS re-porter's response when she questioned me at the airport as we arrived in Greenville. Her statement was, "I hear you're going to be leaving for Mexico this Saturday." To this I said, "Yes, and this time with my wife." The reporter looked at me as if I had told her I was going to the moon, and she began to cry. I said, "If God can take care of me in Haiti, He can certainly take care of me in Mexico!" How often does one get to tell something like that to a secular reporter? God's purpose is always good!

Chapter 51

🕊

MIRACLES

When we turn to the New Testament, we encounter events that meet all the requirements of being called miracles. A miracle is "an effect or extraordinary event in the physical world that surpasses all known human or natural powers and is ascribed to a supernatural cause; or such an effect or event manifesting or considered as a work of God."[1]

These events are also the things that the unbelieving world wants to explain away because their rejection of God forces them to reject also the reality of the spiritual realm. The normal process of cause and effect eliminates for them the possibility that what usually happens can be bypassed by a Higher Power. In this chapter, I want to point out events in the Bible for which there is no human explanation— only God can do what was done in each of these miracles.

I should also point out that civil law requires that there be actual witnesses to any event over which there is debate or disagreement. To report what you heard someone else say or to have been just in the vicinity of the event does not hold up in a court of law. Every miracle that is recorded in the Bible has witnesses, and in some cases

---

1 Dictionary.com/browse/miracle

there were thousands of people who personally witnessed the event. I have also picked out only miracles that are recorded in at least two of the Gospel accounts.

Let's begin with the incarnation and virgin birth of our Savior. Three of the Gospel accounts (Matthew 1:18-25; Luke 1:26-35; John 1:1-2, 14) make it clear, each from a different vantage point, that Christ's birth was a miracle that only God could do. Read what Luke, a physician, says about this miracle:

> *The angel said unto her, Fear not, Mary, for thou hast found favor with God. And behold, thou shalt conceive in thy womb and bring forth a son ... Then said Mary unto the angel, How shall this be, seeing I know not a man. And the angel answered and said unto her, The Holy Ghost shall come upon thee, **and the power of the Highest shall overshadow thee**: therefore also that holy thing which shall be born of thee shall be called the Son of God.*

How clearly does this doctor, along with Matthew and John, certify the virgin birth and make it known that Christ was born of a virgin—a miracle!

The next miracle is at the baptism of Jesus by John the Baptist. All four Gospel accounts record the miraculous event that occurred when the Son of God was baptized (Matthew 3:13-17; Mark 1:9-11; Luke 3:21-22; John 1:31-34).

The Holy Ghost descended in a bodily shape like a dove upon him, and a voice came from heaven, which said, Thou art my beloved Son; in thee I am well pleased (Luke 3:22).

There were many other eyewitnesses at that event as well.

In Matthew 8:1-4, Mark 1:40, and Luke 5:12-14, the miraculous healing of a leper by Christ is recorded. It is also noteworthy that both Matthew and Luke write that there were "great multitudes" that were eyewitnesses to this miracle. There are other statements that indicate there were many witnesses to the miracles: "the whole city," "scribes and Pharisees," "many publicans and sinners," and "all the people were amazed."

Another thing that indicates the veracity of the miracles were the "mysteries" that are mentioned concerning the life and ministry of Christ while He was on the earth. The Scofield Bible, in one of its references, defines a mystery this way: "A mystery in Scripture is a previously hidden truth, now divinely revealed, but in which a supernatural element still remains despite the revelation (p. 1014, note on Matthew 13:11). The Gospel of Matthew records seven mysteries (Matthew 13:1-52).

The last two miracles I want to point out are the feeding of the four thousand and the feeding of the five thousand with extremely limited supplies. A wise saying is that "when God wants to do something good, He starts with the difficult; when He wants to do something great, He starts with the *impossible*." That is exactly what happened in both of these events. With the five thousand men (plus women and children) He began with "five loaves and two fish." With the four thousand men (plus women and children) He began with "seven loaves" and "a few small fish" to feed them. The loaves were small, like what we know as pita bread.

My question for the agnostics would be: "How can you fool that many people into thinking they had enough to eat when there was so little food with which to begin?" Would it be possible to hypnotize that many people? At these events they were not only eyewitnesses, but "eating" witnesses as well.

In considering the large number of miracles that our Lord did in a very short amount of time, the Apostle John's powerful declaration at the close of his Gospel account is appropriate here:

> *And there are many other things which Jesus did, the which, if they should be written every one, I suppose that even the world itself could not contain the books that should be written. Amen* (John 21:25).

Chapter 52

PLEASANT SURPRISES

As I come to the last chapter in this book, I am seeking to look through *the lens of God* as I evaluate events and as news of previous events comes to my attention that are not *little things*. I am personally surprised and overwhelmed as people write to me, or tell me, of some way that the Lord has enabled me to encourage or influence them in their service for the Lord. If you too have served the Lord for some years, you will get the same kind of feedback—either here or in Glory.

Let me begin with something that began in 2013 for me (giving a little more information about something I mentioned in Chapter 40). Dr. David Yearick, the former pastor of a church here in Greenville, called me on a Monday morning in November 2013. He wanted to inform me that he and his wife, Bobbie, had invited three young ladies who visited their church to their house for lunch. He said he asked them how they came to BJU.

One young lady said she was from Colombia, South America. Pastor Yearick then asked, "How did you ever hear about BJU?" She said she was listening to a man named Frank Garlock speaking on the radio about music when she was about twelve years old, and when he mentioned BJU, she decided right there that if she ever went to college, she was going to go to that university. Dr. Yearick then said, "I know Frank Garlock. He is a friend of mine." In surprise she said, "You know Frank Garlock?!"

Upon hearing this, I asked Pastor Yearick to get a message to her and tell her that an old couple wanted to meet her. We met her on campus, put her on our prayer list, and during the next couple of years we took her out to dinner several times. However, she evidently ran out of money and had to go to Ohio where her family was living at that time.

The girl's name is Maria Quijano, and about three weeks ago we were surprised to meet her at Shepherd's Care where we live, and she is graduating this year as an outstanding nursing major. She has also been accepted at the Clinical Cardiology Section of the prestigious Cleveland Clinic, one of the best heart hospitals in the world.

For a more recent incident, I met a man named David Tessmann two weeks ago; he first told me and then came by where we live to show me what he has written about something that happened years ago. When he was the pastor at the Bethlehem Baptist Church in Viroqua, Wisconsin, a group of twelve hippies who were revolting against their wealthy parents came to visit his church. They had been invited there by one of the church's businessmen who had befriended one of the hippies. Pastor Tessmann mentioned φαρμακεία, *pharmakeia*: the use of drugs or spells as in Galatians 5:20, where it means idolatry, sorcery, or witchcraft. The leader of the hippie community invited him to come to their pad and explain what the Greek means. As a result, the leader, his wife, and several other hippies trusted Christ as their Savior

That same hippie had a rock band, so he thought he could use that music for the Lord by changing the name of his band to *The Holy Ghost Band*. However, his renewed conscience was bothering him about using that music for the Lord, so Brother Tessmann gave him a copy of a book I wrote in 1970, *The Big Beat: A Rock Blast*. What I wrote in that book convinced him that he needed to change his music as well as his lifestyle, and he is now the pastor of a fundamental Baptist church in California.

For my next illustration, I will mention just one of the many letters, notes, phone calls, and messages I am currently receiving that reveal to me how God is still working. I will quote from a hand-written note that I received just this week.

> *I have been contemplating writing you for a long time—so, here it is! I have always appreciated your creative leadership musically—your songs, your choral and congregational directing, and your energy! Thank you for presenting to us a distinctive style of music with such substantial life. Mrs. Garlock also set the standard for many on the piano. Thank you for giving us such a wealth and variety of gospel hymns, songs, and seasonal cantatas.*

Just today (April 28, 2018), I met a young lady who is serving the Lord in her church and teaching music even though she has a strange disease and is crippled. Her mother told me that the Patch the Pirate series is what has gotten her daughter through the rough times that she has experienced in growing up with a lot of pain. Her testimony is vibrant and a rich blessing to everyone she meets. She was a blessing to me today.

In thinking about pleasant surprises, I must mention two unusual ones. Since I was ordained in 1952, I have performed many weddings. The last two that I did were in 2013 and 2014, and both of them were exceptional. Number one was for a couple who were each 60 years old and wanted to get married. The man had even asked the lady's father for permission to date her, and although her pastor thought they had not known each other long enough, I agreed to perform the ceremony after counseling them. Ron is a counselor and Kate is a nurse and they are now happily married and serving the Lord together.

Wedding number two is even more unusual. The man and woman had been living together for several years and now had a four-year-old boy. They both said they are Christians and when the boy started asking questions, they knew they should be married as a testimony to their son and their neighbors. Again, after several counseling sessions, I agreed to perform the ceremony in their home. It was attended by eight people including their boy who was the ring bearer for the couple. I met them in a restaurant a couple of years ago, and they were rejoicing that their son is now in a Christian school and how thankful they are that I had done the wedding for them.

For my last illustration, I want to close this book with something that my daughter, Gina, just told me as we are visiting her in Navarre, Florida. She has always had visions of things she loves and would like to be able to do. Several of those "dreams" have not come true the way she thought they might, but they have come in the way God had them planned.

Number one is that she always wanted to live near a beach because she loves the water. If you have read what Gina wrote for *Just Show Up: God Can Use You*, you know of the circumstances that brought Gina and her family to Florida. She is now living right on the water. Her house is on the Intracoastal Waterway that is called "The Sound."

Number two is that she has always had a desire to be a nurse, ever since she was a little girl. She always requested a doctor's kit for birthdays and Christmas. Gina was intimidated in college by the science classes that nursing requires, so she chose another area of study. Her daughter, Torie, is the top student, with a 4.0 average, in the nursing program at the University of Mobile, Alabama, and she seems destined to become an outstanding nurse and physical therapist.

Number three is that Gina has musical ability that has been passed on to her through both of her parents, but she didn't want to try to follow in Shelly's footsteps. However, another daughter of hers, Blythe, is both an excellent musician in several areas of music and also a very talented performer in all that she does. Blythe is a member of outstanding musical groups at the University of Mobile and travels extensively representing the Lord and her school.

Number four is that Gina has always loved sports. Many pastors have told me how Gina embarrassed them when Gina was just a little girl at the Wilds, the Christian camp in North Carolina. She would challenge them to a game of Ping-Pong. Gina could slam the ball over the net from below the table where you could not see it coming. She was also a top athlete through high school. However, that has not been a major interest of hers since then.

But now, her youngest son, Gareth, is an outstanding soccer player who has just been voted the outstanding athlete at North Greenville University where he is a student. Here is what Gareth said when he received that award: "I am grateful for the award. I was unaware I had to give a speech, so I'll keep it quick. I have to give all the glory to God for giving me the ability to play soccer and do what I love. I'd like to give thanks to my family, coaches, and teammates for always being there and supporting me." This is just another instance of what may appear to be *little things* that the Lord is giving Gina as she has followed God in the way that He has led her.

It is exciting to realize that the Lord has let Flora Jean and me live long enough to see how He is leading in the lives of our grandchildren and even our great-grandchildren. They are taking the talents and abilities that God has given them and are using them for His glory.

I have no idea of the surprises the Lord may still have for me, but the main "surprise" could be his sudden Second Coming to receive all those who love Him unto Himself. As the Apostle John at the close of the book of Revelation says,

He which testifieth these things saith, Surely I come quickly. Amen.

I say,

Even so, come, Lord Jesus.
Revelation 21:20

APPENDIX 1

GOD MOVES IN A MYSTERIOUS WAY

The title for this extra chapter comes from a poem by William Cowper (Cooper), one of England's greatest poets who wrote hymns as well. A copy of a song that I wrote on Cowper's text is Figure 11 of the Appendix Figures in *Just Show Up: God Can Use You.*

Here is the text of two stanzas of that song:

> *God moves in a mysterious way,*
> *His wonders to perform;*
> *He plants His footsteps in the sea,*
> *And rides upon the storm.*
>
> *Blind unbelief is sure to err,*
> *And scan His work in vain;*
> *God is His own interpreter,*
> *And He will make it plain.*

I am using this extraordinary illustration and making it a chapter of its own on September 8, 2018 because it brings what this book is about right up to date. It demonstrates how our great God is always behind the scenes, even when (and perhaps especially when) we are not aware that He is.

TESTIMONY OF AMY KENT

My parents have been very special people. They have fostered thirty-one children through the state of Nebraska and then adopted three of them when I was twenty-four years old. Danielle and David are African-America twins who just turned sixteen, and Eric just turned twelve. They all came to our home directly from the hospital after birth and have lived with us their whole lives. However, several years after both adoptions were finalized, my dad went to be with the Lord very unexpectedly.

A few years later, Mom and I and the three children moved to Plattsmouth, Nebraska. In Plattsmouth, David was in the community school in a special education classroom, which really helped him start to come out of some of his autistic tendencies. Dani (Danielle) immediately thrived at the First Baptist School. Eric repeated a couple of young grades, so we suspected he might have some learning challenges, but second grade was a tremendous year and we thought he had made a breakthrough. Third grade, however, proved to be a rough year. Mom took him out of school at the end of the first quarter and homeschooled him the rest of the year. It didn't take two weeks into fourth grade to realize he needed more help than she could give; she began praying for answers.

For the last few years, I had been studying music with Dr. Mike Zachary and had come to see him not only as a music teacher but also a godly influence and voice of wisdom in my life for various things. Because of this, I mentioned to him some frustrations I was facing in my job. He recommended that I purchase and read Dr. Garlock's recently-published book entitled *Just Show Up: God Can Use You.* He felt it would be an encouragement to me, and he was right!

From the very first pages I began to feel encouraged as I read the stories of how God had worked through Dr. Garlock in the lives of various people whom he had influenced over the years. When I got to the vignette about Dr. Vaughn and how Hidden Treasure Christian School in Taylors, South Carolina had been started, my eyes lit up. A Christian school for special needs children? We had prayed and wished for that for many years but had never heard about this place or anything like it.

Mom and I immediately started researching the school and area and I called Hidden Treasure right away to get information. All the answers to our questions came back giving us good reason to believe it could work out and would be a good fit for our boys. We started doing the paperwork and found that everything Mom had gotten done in the recent months was essential to put the boys on their waiting list. This is paperwork that can take weeks or months to have completed depending on the schedules of the professionals who do it—evaluations, testing and reporting, etc. There were already around thirty other children ahead of us on the waiting list; if we had had to take time to get everything necessary just to get on that list, the number might have doubled by then. God knew months ahead of us that we needed to do certain things to be ready for something we didn't even know about yet!

Only a few weeks before we learned of Hidden Treasure Christian School, we were told that our Grama (grandmother), who had been living with us, only had up to six months to live. We were concerned that moving halfway across the country during that time would be more than she could handle. But my Pastor encouraged me to make a trip and see the area before making any decisions for sure.

Finishing the book left me with a feeling of wishing I could be one of the lives that had intersected with Dr. Garlock the way those in each chapter had. What a blessing to be directly impacted by such a godly man! Our family had been blessed over the years through Majesty Music and other similar ministries and appreciation for Dr. Garlock and all those involved welled up within me so strongly that I wrote a note and sent it to Dr. Garlock. I thanked him for his indirect influence in my life, which I valued so deeply, and explained about finding Hidden Treasure Christian School through his book and mentioned that I would love to meet him while visiting there if possible. I was elated a few weeks later when I received his autobiography in the mail and a personal letter inviting me to contact him when we came to visit so that we could meet each other.

In February we made the trip to Taylors to tour the school, attend church, tour the Logos Theater and attend "Prince Caspian," and look for housing and jobs. I also had the wonderful opportunity to meet Dr. and Mrs. Garlock and they generously took us out for lunch. Having Dr. Garlock ask me questions about my master's degree and tell us stories about his life and how God had been at work throughout everything that had happened was definitely a highlight of the trip. And before I left, Dr. Garlock asked if I would write a piano accompaniment for his choral arrangement of "God Moves in A Mysterious Way." I was thrilled to get this opportunity.

Mom had been constantly reminding us of a two-part theme that the Lord put on her heart back in December. The first part comes from Proverbs 3:5-6, especially the phrase, "lean not unto thine own understanding." The second part was the phrase, "One day at a time," (Matthew 6:34). We knew that this was a God-sized move and it was absolutely impossible for us to make it happen. Therefore, we were completely dependent on Him for wisdom and understanding *literally for each day.* This was not the kind of event that could be planned and scheduled according to our understanding and done in our own power because we had no control over almost everything that was happening.

First, there was Grama's health. We knew the only trip she wanted to take was to her heavenly home. Since we didn't know when that would be, we lived one day at a time, trusting God to give us wisdom for that day and that day alone. This is how it went until May 16th. On that evening, the family gathered around and sang hymns. Then as Allan, my brother-in-law, was reading Jesus' words about preparing a place in Heaven and coming back to receive His people, we watched as Grama left our world and went to be with Jesus.

Second, it was not up to us whether the school would have openings for both boys or not. The typical timeframe for the school to know if there would be openings for new students for the upcoming year was March or April. I think I called three times in those two months to see if they had any news for us. In May I called several more times. The exercise of trusting God was harder that month! By June we had quit calling and just believed that when it was the right time, God would make it happen and we would find out about it at some point. It was the middle of June when we got word that there was probably a place for David, but the younger classes had already filled up and unless something changed, Eric would probably not be able to attend. This was ironic since he was the one in need of a school to begin with.

And third, there was the question of how to sell our house and buy a house (or find somewhere to live temporarily) over a thousand miles away! The day after we put our house on the market, we had an offer at our price, but it was contingent on the buyers selling their house. It was great news and terrible news at the same time. Our agent recommended we give them two weeks to have their house that was pending or else we would move on with trying to sell it to someone else.

Every day of those two weeks felt like an eternity as we now prayed not only for our house to sell but for their house to sell as well. In the meantime, we knew we only had a small window of time to find a house in Taylors and put an offer on it, so we spent every minute looking at new listings and praying that God would make it clear when we had found the right one. A week and a half into our two-week deadline, a house in Wildflower Meadows, a subdivision in Taylors, became available at the right price, the right size, and the right location. Many houses that went on the market went back off the market very quickly—sometimes within the same day—and this looked like a house that wouldn't last long. We didn't want to lose what seemed like the only potential house, but we couldn't make an offer on it until we knew our house was sold, which was still three long days away. So the prayer requests were piling up—not only to sell our house *and* our buyers' house but that God would keep this new house invisible!

What we did not know was that our buyers had gotten an offer on their house and were working on the paperwork during those last three days. Once we got the word, we made an offer on the Taylors house and a week later we had a place to call our own. Although everything that had happened so far was necessary for making this move, the initial purpose of the move was to put the boys in Hidden Treasure Christian School. It didn't really matter anymore that we still had not

heard from the school; the plan was to go—leave July 10th—
and see what the Lord would do. Trusting Him is as good as
seeing with our own eyes! But finally, the Thursday before we
left, we received the long-awaited paperwork with information for *both* boys!

God's timing was much different than what we had hoped
for or would have planned, however, this was more than just
about moving. This was about watching God part the waters
and make a way. This was about the all-powerful God working in the lives of His people who have no strength or power
of their own. This was about our growing in faith and His
getting all the glory!

A special blessing is that Amy is now a Teacher's Assistant at the
Hidden Treasure school.

APPENDIX 2

I am adding one more current event to this book to verify the fact that our great, almighty God is still working today, September 22, 2018. Flora Jean and I have moved to Navarre, Florida to live with Gina and David Greene, our youngest daughter and her husband. Shepherd's Care in Greenville, SC, believed that they could not keep Flora Jean and me there in the way we had enrolled because Flora Jean wanted to move all around the building because of her mental status. That would have meant having us move to "Memory Care" where the situation was not acceptable because Flora Jean can still think and talk even though her memory is short.

Therefore, our family all agreed that we needed to find another solution to the problem. That solution was to move to the Greene's house and live with them. They live right on the Intracoastal Waterway, they have an office for me, a lovely bedroom for us with a fantastic view, and David has built a large porch off our room for Flora Jean to enjoy. The situation is more than we ever could have hoped for.

However, all of the above is not the reason for this second version of "God Moves in a Mysterious Way." Something happened today that shows that the Lord still works His sovereign will in ways that can only be attributed to Him. This is an event that has taken place in which all the diverse strands that have come together could not have come in any other way but by the grace of God (Romans 8:28).

Let me explain. We arrived here two days ago. This afternoon, a man who loves to fish off the Greene's dock appeared with his mature "girlfriend" who happens to be an obstetrician. After being introduced, I followed the fisherman out onto the dock to learn his method of fishing since I have never been a fisherman and I would love to learn how to catch some fish for us to eat.

At the same time, another friend of the Greene's and ours who is a nurse arrived. She is in this area to see her parents who are in a nursing home close by. She is also a close friend of Gina and just stopped by to visit her. While I was on the dock, she struck up a conversation with the doctor. They found they had both worked at the same hospital at different times and had many common medical friends.

As they were now alone the doctor then revealed to our friend that she is being treated for cancer and is concerned for her life. This opened the opportunity for our friend to share the gospel with her, which she received with gladness. She then trusted Christ as her Savior on the lawn overlooking the water. When I came off the dock and approached the two ladies, the doctor readily explained to me what she had done and the three of us rejoiced together that she had become a child of God.

Think about all the various strands that had to come together for this to take place. We had to move from Greenville, SC to Navarre, Florida in order for me to distract the fisherman so that the Christian nurse could gain the confidence of the doctor in order to talk to her about salvation. Was it a happenstance that the nurse came by the Greene's house for a visit at the same time the doctor came? Was their common experience at the same hospital a coincidence for the doctor to be willing to listen to the nurse? Did the doctor's physical problems open the door for a serious conversation just by chance? Who was working in the hearts of these two ladies for the one to sense the other's needs and for the other one to receive the gospel so readily? Was it an accidental thing that the nurse's parents needed the daughter's attention so that she was in Florida instead being at her home in Illinois? Was my desire to learn how to fish so that the two ladies could be left alone incidental? Did God know that this was going to take place today when our daughter and we became friends with the nurse many years ago?

Since this whole book has been about the *Little Things* that our sovereign God is in charge of as He works His omniscient will, this current event illustrates that He never changes, and He is eager to save anyone who will trust in His saving power. I do not know anything about the doctor's background, but I do know that when I gave her my autobiography, she immediately began to read it to her friends who were there as she obviously rejoiced in what the Lord did for her as she read what the Lord has done for me over the years since I trusted Him as a five-year-old boy. As you read this, will you rejoice with me in the overwhelming power of our great God to control the *Little Things* of our lives? Will you recognize that we must look through the lens of God to understand the circumstances, and not let the circumstances distort your view of God?

www.ingramcontent.com/pod-product-compliance
Lightning Source LLC
LaVergne TN
LVHW041249080426
835510LV00009B/648